First World War
and Army of Occupation
War Diary
France, Belgium and Germany

60 DIVISION
Divisional Troops
Royal Army Service Corps
Divisional Train (517,518,519,520 Companies A.S.C.)
23 June 1915 - 30 November 1916

WO95/3029/8

The Naval & Military Press Ltd
www.nmarchive.com
Published in association with The National Archives

Published by

The Naval & Military Press Ltd

Unit 10 Ridgewood Industrial Park,

Uckfield, East Sussex,

TN22 5QE England

Tel: +44 (0) 1825 749494

www.naval-military-press.com

www.nmarchive.com

This diary has been reprinted in facsimile from the original. Any imperfections are inevitably reproduced and the quality may fall short of modern type and cartographic standards.

© Crown Copyright
Images reproduced by permission of The National Archives, London, England, 2015.

Contents

Document type	Place/Title	Date From	Date To
Heading	WO95/3029/7		
Heading	60th Division Divl Train A.S.C. (517 520 Coys ASC) 1915 June To 1916 Nov		
War Diary	Butts,farm Feltham Middlesex	23/06/1915	24/06/1915
War Diary	Harlow	25/06/1915	31/08/1915
Miscellaneous	General Staff Co (London) Division	08/09/1915	08/09/1915
War Diary	Saffron Walden	10/09/1915	23/09/1915
War Diary	Bishop's Stortford	01/09/1915	02/10/1915
War Diary	Saffron Walden	09/10/1915	22/10/1915
War Diary	Bishops Stortford	27/10/1915	27/10/1915
War Diary	Hatfield Broad Oak Essex	02/10/1915	02/10/1915
War Diary	Sittlebury Essex	31/10/1915	31/10/1915
Miscellaneous	Headquarters Co (London) Division	05/10/1915	05/10/1915
Miscellaneous	Headquarters Co (London) Division	05/11/1915	05/11/1915
War Diary	Bishops Stortford	01/11/1915	30/11/1915
War Diary	Littlebury Essex	01/11/1915	30/11/1915
War Diary	Bishops Stortford	01/11/1915	29/11/1915
War Diary	Braintree Essex	02/12/1915	02/12/1915
Heading	War Diary Of 1 South Infantry Brigade Co Asc From 1st December 1915 To 31st December 1915 Volume 2 No. 12		
War Diary	Littlebury	01/12/1915	31/12/1915
Heading	War Diary Of 179th Infantry Brigade Train Company From 1st December 1915 Is The 31st December 1915 Volume 2 No. 12		
War Diary	Bishops Stortford	20/12/1915	31/12/1915
War Diary	Bishop's Stortford	01/12/1915	19/12/1915
Miscellaneous	Inspection By G.O.C. 60th London Division		
Heading	War Diary Of No. 4 Company A.S.C. 60th (London) Divisional Train From 1st December 1915 To 31st December 1915 Volume 2 No. 12		
War Diary	Braintree	01/12/1915	31/12/1915
Heading	War Diary Of Headquarters Company 60th (Lond) Divl. Train From 1st Decr To 31st Decr 1915 Volume 2 No.12		
War Diary	Bishops Stortford	02/12/1915	31/12/1915
Heading	War Diary Of The 180th Infantry Brigade Train Coy From Feb-1-1916 To Feb-29-1916 Volume III No. 2		
War Diary	Warminster	01/02/1916	29/02/1916
Miscellaneous	Inspection Of Transport Of This Company By Major General 7.W.B London C.B		
War Diary	Warminster	01/02/1916	29/02/1916
Miscellaneous	Inspection Of Transport Of This Company By Major General 7.W.B. London C.B		
Heading	War Diary No. 4 Coy 60th (London) Divisional Train From 1st March 1916 To 31st March 1916		
War Diary	Warminster	01/03/1916	31/03/1916
Heading	War Diary Of The 519 Coy A.S.C From 1st March 1916 To 31st March 1916 Volume III No. 3		
War Diary	Warminster	01/03/1916	31/03/1916

Heading	War Diary Of 520th (H.T) Co. A.S.C. 60th (London) Divisional Train From 1st April 1916 To 30th April 1916		
War Diary	Warminster	01/04/1916	30/04/1916
Heading	War Diary Of The 519th Coy A.S.C From April 1st 1916 To April 30th 1916 Volume III		
War Diary	Warminster	01/04/1916	30/04/1916
Heading	War Diary Of 520th (H.T) Co. A.S.C. 60th (London) Divisional Train From 1st May 1916 To 31st May 1916		
War Diary	Warminster	01/05/1916	31/05/1916
War Diary	Warminster	24/05/1916	31/05/1916
Heading	War Diary of the 519th H.T. Coy. A.S.C. From June 1st 1916 To June 21st 1916 Volume III No. 6		
War Diary	Warminster	01/06/1916	21/06/1916
Heading	War Diary 520th (H.T.) Co. A.S.C. 60th (London) Divisional Train 1st June 1916 To 30th Col June 1916		
War Diary	Warminster	01/06/1916	24/06/1916
Heading	War Diary of 60th (London) Divisional A.S.C. From 20th June 1916 To 30th June 1916 Volume I No. (1)		
War Diary	Warminster	20/06/1916	24/06/1916
War Diary	Train Hdqrs	23/06/1916	23/06/1916
War Diary	Flers	24/06/1916	30/06/1916
Miscellaneous	Appendix I. Order of Embarkation 60th Division.		
Miscellaneous	Overseas Move Appendix II		
Miscellaneous	Overseas Rations Appendix II (b)		
Miscellaneous	Appendix III	25/06/1916	25/06/1916
Miscellaneous	Appendix IV Groups For Refilling 27th		
Miscellaneous	Supply Groupling For Refilling On The 28th		
Miscellaneous	Appendix VI Supply Grouping For Refilling On The 29th	28/06/1916	28/06/1916
Heading	War Diary of 60th (London) Divisional A.S.C. From 1st July 1916 To 31st July 1916 Volume I No. 2		
War Diary	Tinques	01/07/1916	15/07/1916
War Diary	Hermaville	16/07/1916	20/07/1916
War Diary	Haute Avesnes	21/07/1916	31/07/1916
Miscellaneous	List Of Units Of The 60th Division. Appendix I		
Miscellaneous	Appendix II	28/06/1916	28/06/1916
Miscellaneous	Refilling Points on 1st July 1916 Appendix III	30/06/1916	30/06/1916
Miscellaneous	Appendix IV		
Miscellaneous	Appendix V C.R.E.	07/07/1916	07/07/1916
Miscellaneous	Appendix VI Subject Refilling Points.	14/07/1916	14/07/1916
Miscellaneous	Appendix VII. Allotements Of Wagons.	15/07/1916	15/07/1916
Miscellaneous	O.C. 1.2.3. and 4 Companies. 60th Divisional Train.	15/07/1916	15/07/1916
Miscellaneous	D.D.S. & T. III Army.	07/07/1915	07/07/1915
Miscellaneous	War Establishments A Divisional Train		
Miscellaneous	60th Division Location Return Appendix VIII		
Miscellaneous	Appendix VIIIA H.Q. XVII Corps.	17/07/1916	17/07/1916
Miscellaneous	To. O.C. 1,2.3.4. Coys. 60th Div. Train. Appendix IX	22/07/1916	22/07/1916
Miscellaneous	Distribution Of Baggage Wagons. Table A.		
Miscellaneous	Table "C"		
Heading	War Diary of 60th London Div Train From 1st August 1916 To 31st August 1916 Volume I No. 3		
War Diary	Haute Avesnes	01/08/1916	31/08/1916
Miscellaneous	Appendix I.		
Miscellaneous	War Diary August 1916 60th London Divl Train Appendix II		

Miscellaneous	War Diary August 1916 60th. (London) Divisional Train Appendix III	22/07/1916	22/07/1916
Miscellaneous	E.F. Wagons No. 1 Coy		
Miscellaneous	Appendix IV	16/08/1916	16/08/1916
Miscellaneous	War Diary 60th. (London) Divisional Train. Appendix 7	21/08/1916	21/08/1916
Miscellaneous	Headquarters Company - Group "A"		
Miscellaneous	No. 2. Company 60th. Divl. Train Group "B"		
Miscellaneous	No. 3 Company. 60th Divl. Train. Group "C"		
Miscellaneous	No. 4 Company 60th Divl. Train. Group "D"		
Miscellaneous	War Diary 60th London Divl Train Aug 1916 Appendix VI	16/08/1916	16/08/1916
Miscellaneous	War Diary August 1916 60 London Divisional Train Appendix VII		
Miscellaneous	War Diary-Appendix VIII		
Miscellaneous	Vegetables bought for 60th Division during the month of August 1916 by Q. 293 60th Divisional Train. Appendix IX		
Heading	War Diary of 60th London Divisional Train From 1st September 1916 To 30th September 1916 Volume No. 4		
War Diary	Haute Avesnes	01/09/1916	30/09/1916
Miscellaneous	War Diary 60 London Div Train September 1916 Appendix I		
Miscellaneous	War Diary 60 London Divl Train Appendix II	01/09/1916	01/09/1916
Miscellaneous	War Diary 60 London Divl Train Appendix III	16/08/1916	16/08/1916
Miscellaneous	War Diary 60th London Divisional Train September 1916 Appendix IV	19/08/1916	19/08/1916
Miscellaneous	War Diary 60th. (London) Divisional Train. September 1916. No. 2. Company 60th. Divl. Train. Group "B" Appendix IV.		
Miscellaneous	War Diary 60th. (London) Divisional Train. September 1916	19/08/1916	19/08/1916
Miscellaneous	60th (London) Divisional Train September 1916 Appendix V	16/09/1916	16/09/1916
Miscellaneous	War Diary 60th (London) Divisional A.S.C. Appendix V		
Miscellaneous	War Diary 60th. London Divl Train. Appendix VI		
Miscellaneous	War Diary 60 London Div Train Appendix VII	25/09/1916	25/09/1916
Miscellaneous	War Diary 60 Lond. Div. Train September 1916 Appendix VII		
Miscellaneous	War Diary 60 Div Train Sept 1916 Appendix VIII		
Miscellaneous	War Diary - 60th. (London) Divisional Train. September 1916 Appendix IX		
Miscellaneous	War Diary - 60th. (London) Divisional Train.September 1916 Appendix X	02/10/1916	02/10/1916
Heading	War Diary of 60th London Divl Train 1st October 1916 To 31st October 1916 Volume I No. 5		
War Diary	Haute Avesnes	01/10/1916	27/10/1916
War Diary	Houvin	22/10/1916	27/10/1916
War Diary	Frohen Le Petit	28/10/1916	29/10/1916
War Diary	Bernauville	29/10/1916	31/10/1916
Miscellaneous	Appendix I		
Miscellaneous	Subject:- Refilling Points. Appendix		
Miscellaneous			
Miscellaneous	Subject Re-grouping Refilling. Transport. Appendix III	25/09/1916	25/09/1916

Miscellaneous	Time Table for Loading at Railhead and for Refilling at Dumps.	25/09/1916	25/09/1916
Miscellaneous	Appendix IV		
Miscellaneous	O.C. 1.2,3.4, Cos. 60th Train Appendix V	13/10/1916	13/10/1916
Diagram etc	Appendix VI		
Miscellaneous	Regrouping with effect from the 18th Oct 1916 Appendix VI (a)		
Miscellaneous	Appendix VII Headquarters, 179th Infty Bde. Appendix VII	21/10/1916	21/10/1916
Miscellaneous	60th Divisional Train Order No. 1 Appendix VIII		
Miscellaneous	Table "A" Position Of Units During Relief		
Miscellaneous	Table "D"		
Miscellaneous	Grouping 24.10.16 To 28.10.16		
Miscellaneous	60th London Divisional Train Order No. 2 Appendix XI		
Miscellaneous	Table "A"		
Miscellaneous	60th London Divl. Train Order No. 3 Appendix XII		
Miscellaneous	Appendix XIII. Grouping 9.1.16	09/10/1916	09/10/1916
Heading	War Diary of 60th Divl Train From 1st November 1916 To 30th November 1916 Vol 2 No. 6		
War Diary	Bernaville	01/11/1916	04/11/1916
War Diary	Ailly Le Haut Clocher	06/11/1916	29/11/1916
War Diary	Salonika	30/11/1916	30/11/1916
Miscellaneous	60th Divisional Train Order No. 5. Appendix II	02/11/1916	02/11/1916
Miscellaneous	60th (London) Divisional A.S.C. Appendix 2	05/11/1916	05/11/1916
Miscellaneous	War Diary 60th (London) Divisional A.S.C. Appendix 3	05/11/1916	05/11/1916
Miscellaneous	A Form Messages And Signals.		
Miscellaneous	H.Q. 179th Infy Bde.	04/11/1916	04/11/1916
Miscellaneous	H.Q. 179th Infy. Bde. Appendix 4	06/11/1916	06/11/1916
Miscellaneous	Appendix 5. 60th (London) Divisional. A.S.C. Appendix 5		

WO 95/3029/7

60TH DIVISION

DIVL TRAIN A.S.C.

(517-520 Coys ASC)

1915 JUNE to 1916 NOV.

Army Form C. 2118.

CO DIV TRAIN

WAR DIARY
INTELLIGENCE SUMMARY
(Erase heading not required.)

Instructions regarding War Diaries and Intelligence Summaries are contained in F.S. Regs., Part II. and the Staff Manual respectively. Title pages will be prepared in manuscript.

Hour, Date, Place	Summary of Events and Information	Remarks and references to Appendices
10.32 a.m. Wed. June 23 1915. BUTTS FARM. FELTHAM. MIDDLESEX.	The 2/2 County of London (9) Advanced party of two officers (Captain BOWATER. T.D.B. & 2/Lt. PATERSON.R.J.) left by train for HARLOW. ESSEX - arriving at 2.44 p.m. JS	
7 a.m. Thurs. June 24 1915. Same place.	The mounted party of the above mentioned Unit thirteen officers, one hundred & fifty eight men, one hundred & sixty nine horses, eighteen motor cyclists, three transport wagons, the whole under the command of Lt. Col. Sir SIMEON STUART. Bart. left by route march via HOUNSLOW - BRENTFORD - LONDON. EPPING. to HARLOW. arriving at 6.30 p.m. Halts were made to water & feed at SERPENTINE. HYDE PARK. 10.30 a.m. and EPPING at 5.15 p.m. All thirteen horses arrived in excellent condition. JS	

(9 29 6) W 2794 100,000 8/14 H W V Forms/C. 2118/11

Army Form C. 2118.

WAR DIARY
or
INTELLIGENCE SUMMARY.
(Erase heading not required.)

Hour, Date, Place	Summary of Events and Information	Remarks and references to Appendices
4.30 a.m. Thurs June 24th 1915. Same place.	The dismounted party consisting of five officers and one hundred & thirty-one men, seventeen horses, one transport wagon & twenty tons of baggage & stores marched to HOUNSLOW Station L. & S.W. Railway & entrained, leaving at 7.25 a.m. for HARLOW arriving at 9.40 a.m. The officers & men to take up billets arranged on the 23rd. by the advanced party & by 9.30 a.m. the whole unit with exception of Rear guard left at FELTHAM to hand in stores were comfortably housed & fed. AS	
June 25 1915. HARLOW.	Various Orders from G.O.C. 2/2 LONDON DIVISION received & acted on as to Regimental Camp. A draft of thirty men from the 3/2 County of LONDON arrived at 10.55 a.m. from H.Q. ELVERTON Street LONDON were taken on the strength of this unit. AS	

3.

Army Form C. 2118.

Instructions regarding War Diaries and Intelligence
Summaries are contained in F. S. Regs., Part II.
and the Staff Manual respectively. Title pages
will be prepared in manuscript.

WAR DIARY
or
INTELLIGENCE SUMMARY.
(Erase heading not required.)

Hour, Date, Place	Summary of Events and Information	Remarks and references to Appendices
Saturday June 26th 1915	Horses were exercised & all arrangements com- pleted for comfort of men & horses. JS	
June 27th 1915	The rear guard consisting of two officers and thirty six N.C.O.'s & men arrived at 5.44 p.m. & were sent to their billets. JS	
June 28th 1915	Regimental drill under the C.O. Thirty one horses joined, one from BISHOPS STORTFORD, 17th City of LONDON Regt. and thirty from AVONMOUTH remount depot SHIREHAMPTON. The latter arrived in Camp at 9.15 p.m. in good condition. An order was received from the G.O.C 2/2 LONDON DIVISION stating that this unit was now attached to the Division & would take their orders accordingly. JS	Regd. No. A/1596/4 June 25th to 19.15. BISHOPS STORTFORD.
June 29th 1915	Regimental drill under the C.O. & the usual carry on. JS	

Army Form C. 2118.

WAR DIARY
or
INTELLIGENCE SUMMARY.
(Erase heading not required.)

4

Hour, Date, Place	Summary of Events and Information	Remarks and references to Appendices
June 29th 15 - HARLOW	One hundred & sixteen rifles were received at 9 p.m. from the TOWER - LONDON.	

June 30th 1915 -	The G.O.C. Brigadier General CALLEY. T.C.P. C.B. M.V.O. inspected this unit at MARKHALL PARK - HARLOW at 2.30 p.m. & visited Regtl lines. Parade State
	
	        Rank & File
	Officers
	Mounted 18 132
	Dismounted 5 250
	        ――― ―――
	Total 23 382
	
	Distribution
	      Officers Rank & File Horses
	On Parade 23 352 Chargers (Public) 4
	Hospital & sick 13 " (Troops) 14
	Attached 4 8 Draft Horses 132
	Leave 2 Attached 3 Transport 9
	       ―― Regtl. Employ 1 438 Attached 3
	       29 Segregated 36	

TNA/219

Army Form C. 2118.

WAR DIARY
or
INTELLIGENCE SUMMARY.
(Erase heading not required.)

Instructions regarding War Diaries and Intelligence Summaries are contained in F.S. Regs., Part II. and the Staff Manual respectively. Title pages will be prepared in manuscript.

Hour, Date, Place	Summary of Events and Information	Remarks and references to Appendices
June 30. h 15. HARLOW. (continued)	At 3.22 p.m. a telegram was received from SEARAIL LONDON ordering draft of one officer 2/Lt REID. J.L. & twenty seventeen other ranks to proceed from HARLOW by the 8.11 a.m. train Thurs. July 1st to ST BUDEAUX, en route to join the 1/2 County of LONDON in EGYPT.	Ref N°s A4897 QMG2 and A4654 QMG2

WAR DIARY
or
INTELLIGENCE SUMMARY.
(Erase heading not required.)

Army Form C. 2118.

Hour, Date, Place	Summary of Events and Information	Remarks and references to Appendices
8-11 a.m. July 1st 1915. HARLOW.	A draft of one officer (2/Lt REID.J.L) + twenty seven rank + file left by rail for ST. BUDEAUX en route to EGYPT to join the 1/2 C° of LONDON.	Ref. Regtl Order 156 July 1st 1915.
10.30 a.m. Same date. Same place	The P.V.S. 3rd ARMY. Col. WALTERS.W.B. C.B. F.R.C.V.S. accompanied by Lt. Col. LANE. A.H. A.D.V.S. 2/2 LONDON DIVISION. inspected the horses of this unit in the Regtl Horse Lines - Strength Officers Chargers 4 Troop Horses 206 Transport - 9 Total 219	
July 2nd 1915. HARLOW	Regimental parade under the 2nd i/c major RODEN.W.T. in the 60 acre field belonging to Mr. JAMES.ANDERSON. FELTIMORES FARM.	

# WAR DIARY or INTELLIGENCE SUMMARY

Army Form C. 2118.

Hour, Date, Place	Summary of Events and Information	Remarks and references to Appendices
July 2nd HQ 1.45pm (?) HARLOW	Capt. ARCHER. B.H. A.P.M. called at 3.45 p.m. with an order from D.A.A + Q.M.G 2/2 LONDON DIVISION - for 1 Sgt. 1 Cpl. + 6 troopers to proceed to BISHOPS. STORTFORD. to be stationed there as M.M.P. An order was received that all Home Service men belonging to this Unit should proceed to COLCHESTER on Tuesday July 6th 1915 to be attached to the 106th PROVISIONAL. BATTALION.	Letter unnumbered D.A.A + Q.M.G 2/7/15 2/2 London Div. Ref. No. A1446/22 2/7/15
3.p.m. July 3rd 15 HARLOW	Major FEGEN. C.M. R.A.M.C (T.F.) Sanitary Officer 2/2 LONDON. DIVISION. inspected the proposed site for a camp by Regt.s Parade Ground.	
July 4th 15 Sunday Same place	Horse Regtl. No. 30 died this date.	

WAR DIARY
or
INTELLIGENCE SUMMARY.
(Erase heading not required.)

Army Form C. 2118.

Instructions regarding War Diaries and Intelligence Summaries are contained in F. S. Regs., Part II. and the Staff Manual respectively. Title pages will be prepared in manuscript.

Hour, Date, Place	Summary of Events and Information	Remarks and references to Appendices
1 p.m. July 5th '15 HARLOW.	One Sergeant. One corporal & 7 men left by route march for BISHOPS. STORTFORD to be attached to the 2/2 LONDON DIVISION as mounted Police. The musketry course which should have commenced at BISHOPS-STORTFORD today postponed on account of harvesting arrangements.	Regt'l Orders No 159 par. 6.
6 a.m. July 6th '15 HARLOW.	One L/Cpl & 54 men (all the Home Service men belonging to this Unit) left by 6 a.m. train for BISHOPS. STORTFORD & there entrained 6 r.£.35 a.m. for COLCHESTER to be attached to the 106th PROVISIONAL. BATTY.	Regt'l Orders 159 par 7 July 5, 5th '15.
July 6th '15. Same Place	Musketry. 2 Officers (2/Lt. BOSTOCK.J.A. and 2/Lt. PATERSON. R.J.) & 6 rank & file left by the 8 a.m. train from HARLOW for BISHOPS. STORTFORD. Order that-men who had not joined	Regt'l Order 158 Ref. July 3rd par 8.

Form C 2118. (9 29 6) W 2704 100,000 8/14 H·W V

WAR DIARY
or
INTELLIGENCE SUMMARY.

(Erase heading not required.)

Army Form C. 2118.

Hour, Date, Place	Summary of Events and Information	Remarks and references to Appendices
July 6th '15. (Con.1d) HARLOW	Their musketry course should do so.	
2.45 pm July 6th '15' Same place	A board assembled to inquire cause of death of those No 30. Verdict "internal haemorrhage" implicated bowel - caused by weather.	Ref Regtl Orders. No 159 p.11 July 5th.
July 7th '15' HARLOW.	Musketry course - Officers Patrols par. Weather very wet - Officers Patrols postponed till Thursday July 8th. 2/L BOSTOCK T.H.G. + two N.C.O's left for BISHOPS STORTFORD by 10.50 am train to be attached to the 2/2 LONDON DIVISIONAL Signal Company R.E. to give instruction in Equitation + horse-mastership.	Ref 2/2 LONDON Dy Orders No 213. Para 3
July 8th '15' HARLOW.	Musketry course continued - Officers Patrols.	Ref Regtl Orders No. 160 July 6th

WAR DIARY
or
INTELLIGENCE SUMMARY.
(Erase heading not required.)

Army Form C. 2118.

Hour, Date, Place	Summary of Events and Information	Remarks and references to Appendices
July 14th 15 HARLOW	Route march - under the O.C. moved off at 8.30 a.m.	Reg'l Orders pro 3. July 13th
July 15th 15 same place	Rifles .303 recalled from Squadrons & 256 Japanese Carbines issued instead	
July 16th 15 same place	Tactical Exercise without troops under the direction of the F.S. 2/2 LONDON Rev'd?	
July 17th 15 same place	Nil	
July 18th 15 HARLOW	BUTTS FARM handed over 3/2 S-E. of LONDON (Cyclists) then left as caretakers withdrawn.	
July 19th 15 Same place	Tactical Exercise without troops under the direction of the F.S. 2/2 LONDON Rev'd?	
July 20th 15 same place	Reg'l Exercise (taking up position) under the C.O. at HARLOW COMMON.	

WAR DIARY
or
INTELLIGENCE SUMMARY.

(Erase heading not required.)

Army Form C. 2118.

Hour, Date, Place	Summary of Events and Information	Remarks and references to Appendices
July 9th '15 HARLOW 10.30 p.m.	Musketry Course continued	
Same date & place	Forty 14 horses principally L.D. received from BISHOPS STORTFORD. taken on to being fit July 10th	Ref W.K. 151. July 9'
July 10th '15	No musketry. Outbreak of Mange Ringworm in the ⅓ of horses received from 29.6.15 Musketry Course completed.	
July 11th '15		
July 12th '15	16 thirty men attached from the 3/2 Co. of LONDON Roving Range turn musketry taken on to the strength of the Regt. Regt Drill under the O.C. 6.30 a.m. Seventeen horses arrived by rail HARLOW Stn G.E.R. at 6.30 p.m. from the 3/2 C.of L	Ref W Reg No Order 165 - pm 6 July 12th
July 13th '15 6.30 p.m.	LONDON	

WAR DIARY or INTELLIGENCE-SUMMARY

Army Form C. 2118.

Hour, Date, Place	Summary of Events and Information	Remarks and references to Appendices
July 20th '15 HARLOW	The outbreak of Mange & Ringworm brought by the theft of horses received on June 29th from Avonmouth greatly increased. Seven cases to-me so better encouraged no doubt by the thirsty & insanitary condition of the stables when the Regt. marched in.	
July 21st '15	Tactical Exercise without troops under the direction of the G.S. 2/2 LONDON DIV.	G.2553/3 14/7/15
July 22nd '15 HARLOW	2/Lt GOODE. H.M. reported in today casually his as many from July 1st.	
July 23rd '15 HARLOW	Capt. IAN DENNISTOUN D.A.A & Q.M.G. arrived 3p.m. at Camp. Horse Lines made definite arrangements re M.M.P. to proceed to BISHOPS. STORTFORD - HATFIELD. BROAD OAK - & SAFFRON. WALDEN - to divisional & Brigade Police WDR.	

WAR DIARY
or
INTELLIGENCE SUMMARY.
(Erase heading not required.)

Army Form C. 2118.

Hour, Date, Place	Summary of Events and Information	Remarks and references to Appendices
5:30 p.m. July 24th 15th HARLOW	The A.D.V.S. Lt. Col. LANE. A.H. 22 LONDON ROAD visited the Regtl Lines & cast. juries & ordered fifteen L.D. horses to be returned Remount Depot BISHOPS STORTFORD.	
July 25th 15th (Sunday) Same place	Nil	
July 26th 15th	15 Horses mentioned above left at 5.15 a.m. for BISHOPS STORTFORD. Regtl Exercise under the C.O. at HARLOW COMMON.	
July 27th 15th HARLOW	The men for M.M.P. for Division & 4th & 5th & 6th "Res" Regt reported 176 Brigades & moved off at 9 a.m. from Barr. 6. July 24.6.) Regtl Horse Lines Regt 1st Exercise under the C.O.	
July 28th 15th HARLOW.		
July 29th 15th HARLOW	5 Horses sold BISHOPS STORTFORD/AAVS. 32 LONDON AV. 270/15al/25/7/15)	

Army Form C. 2118.

WAR DIARY
or
INTELLIGENCE SUMMARY

(Erase heading not required.)

Instructions regarding War Diaries and Intelligence Summaries are contained in F. S. Regs., Part II. and the Staff Manual respectively. Title pages will be prepared in manuscript.

Hour, Date, Place	Summary of Events and Information	Remarks and references to Appendices
July 30th 1915. HARLOW	Nil	
July 31st 1915. Same place	30 un-horsed officers & 30 men received from Remount Dépôt ROMFORD.	

Army Form C. 2118.

WAR DIARY
or
INTELLIGENCE SUMMARY

(Erase heading not required.)

Instructions regarding War Diaries and Intelligence Summaries are contained in F. S. Regs., Part II. and the Staff Manual respectively. Title pages will be prepared in manuscript.

Hour, Date, Place	Summary of Events and Information	Remarks and references to Appendices
August 1st 1915 HARLOW	Nil	
August 2nd 1915 "HARLOW"	Black Transport Gelding N° 30 died at 1.30 p.m. - Septic pneumonia.	
August 3rd 1915 HARLOW	Bay mare from Section N° Montastiek with septic pneumonia.	
Aug 4 1915 HARLOW	Route march via CHAMPIONS - MOTTS GREEN - HATFIELD HEATH - SHEERING - Sir OF LANE. ADVS. of LONDON Dist. visited H. Regt. Horse lines	
Aug 5th 1915 HARLOW	Nil	
Aug 6th 1915 same place	Regtl Drill under the C.O.	
Aug 7th 1915 same place	Nil	
Aug 8th 1915 same place	Nil	

Army Form C. 2118.

WAR DIARY
or
INTELLIGENCE SUMMARY

(Erase heading not required.)

Instructions regarding War Diaries and Intelligence Summaries are contained in F.S. Regs., Part II. and the Staff Manual respectively. Title pages will be prepared in manuscript.

Hour, Date, Place	Summary of Events and Information	Remarks and references to Appendices
Aug 9th 1915. HARLOW	Regt Parade under the C.O. 8.30 a.m.	
2.45 p.m.	Aliens counted. Regt turned out.	
3.35 p.m.	Advance guard moved off	
4 p.m.	main body " "	
4.20 p.m.	Rear guard " "	
5 p.m. Orders rec'd. Regt. return to Camp to		
	Orders received from Div'l Comdr to prepare a draft-s-screen for drenches.	
Aug 10th 1915 HARLOW	1.50 p.m. jeep.	
	3.45 p.m. L.Col. MALCOLM P. H.H.Q.M.G. M.V.O. D.S.O	
	4.40 p.m.	
	4.10 p.m. Major General FORSTER. R.J.B. Comdy. Third Army Central Force. Visits the Regt.	
	Here but inspects to Vind. generally including musketry Classes.	
	C.O. 2nd Lt. HODGKINSON. machine gun officer at CHELMSFORD- Lecture to machine gun Sec's.	
Aug 11th 1915 HARLOW	Tactical scheme under the C.O. Lt. SIMEON STUART. M.	

WAR DIARY
or
INTELLIGENCE SUMMARY

(Erase heading not required.)

Army Form C. 2118.

Hour, Date, Place	Summary of Events and Information	Remarks and references to Appendices
Aug 12th 1915 HARLOW	Nil	
Aug 13th 1915 same place	Nil	
Aug 14th 1915 same place	11.15 am. 54 by riding horses arrived at Ref CENTRAFORCE M⁄r HARLOW R⁄y Station from Remount Depot Q1707 Aug 12/h. ORMSKIRK. 10.20 pm. 54 pack horses arrived from 2/1 S.M.D. Branch Veterinary Hospital P⁄of L⁄m⁄ Division V 4461/15 CHELMSFORD. Aug 13 K. 15. Lt. FAGAN. H. R.A.M.C.(T.F) reports t.c.o.	
Aug 15th 1915 same place	Nil	
Aug 16th 1915 same place.	Lt. FAGAN. H. looks over the duties of medical officer to this unit.	
Aug 17th 1915 same place	Draft were received into the depot - received Ref - 236 A.G.(2a) 17 & 12 noon W.p. 19.6.	

Army Form C. 2118.

WAR DIARY
or
INTELLIGENCE SUMMARY
(Erase heading not required.)

Instructions regarding War Diaries and Intelligence Summaries are contained in F.S. Regs., Part II. and the Staff Manual respectively. Title pages will be prepared in manuscript.

Hour, Date, Place	Summary of Events and Information	Remarks and references to Appendices
Aug 18th 1915. HARLOW	Outposts scheme - in the direction of HARLOW + LATTON COMMONS. under Major HIGGIN H.C. Wire received from H.O.C. ADMINISTRATIVE CENTRE stating 2/2 County of LONDON completed that all recruits would now be sent to their unit.	Reg¹ Order Aug 17/15 gr. X. or 19 S. par. 3
Aug 19th 1915 same place	2¹ Col¹ Currie attended at the H.Q. ELVERTON ST. WESTMINSTER to confer with the O.C. ADMINISTRATIVE CENTRE re all recruits & notices sent to the Battery sent 1 - to the 2/2 Co. of LONDON. Orders received that the Draft under Orders to OVERSEAS will entrain on Sunday Aug 22nd at 6.45 am G.E.R. HARLOW Station	Ref A7875 Q.M.G 2.
Aug 20th 1915 same place 9.5 pm	Reg¹ Route March under its C.O. Wire received cancelling move of Draft.	Ref Reg¹ Orders N°14 par 5. Aug 19th/15 Ref A7942 QMG 2.

Army Form C. 2118.

WAR DIARY
or
INTELLIGENCE SUMMARY
(Erase heading not required.)

Instructions regarding War Diaries and Intelligence Summaries are contained in F. S. Regs., Part II. and the Staff Manual respectively. Title pages will be prepared in manuscript.

Hour, Date, Place	Summary of Events and Information	Remarks and references to Appendices
Aug 21st '15. HARLOW	Orders received that this Unit will form a CAMP on the same site as the Reg. at Home. Lines are NORTH of MARK HALL PARK — on the South side. Information received That 150 more horses were to be sent to this Unit.	Ref Q. 177/61 of LONDON DIST. Aug 20th
Aug 22nd '15 same place	Nil.	
Aug 23rd '15 same place	The Divisional Sanitary Officer visited the Reg. Lines at 3.30 p.m. in order to inspect & report upon the purposes site for the CAMP.	
Aug 24th '15 same place	OPPENHEIM 179 Brigade Staff Capt. gave a reclamation of thirty two horses a & R. received at the Reg. Hd Head Quarters. Orders received That (1) The Post prepared departure of the OVERSEAS Draft to would take Place on Aug 26th at 10.40 p.m from HARLOW G.E.R.

WAR DIARY or INTELLIGENCE SUMMARY

Army Form C. 2118.

(Erase heading not required.)

Instructions regarding War Diaries and Intelligence Summaries are contained in F. S. Regs., Part II. and the Staff Manual respectively. Title pages will be prepared in manuscript.

Hour, Date, Place	Summary of Events and Information	Remarks and references to Appendices
Aug 25th '15 HARLOW	Regt mobilized and C.O. HARLOW LATTON COMMONS. Programme:— 10 p.m. 50 NH horses R2. arrived via BISHOPS STORTFORD from SHIREHAMPTON — were picqueted out in his lines tent.	Ref A.D.V.S. wire Aug 25 No V.2.63.
Aug 26th '15 Same place	Major HAWORTH L. Pvts 63 R & N Horselines & Selected a site to prepare camp. Ref:- Americas. 20 officers (Mr PATERSON J.Sgt 79/1st BOSTOCK J.M.L.) + 55 N.C.O's men billetted to Sr BUDEAUX Rest Camp. 10.45 p.m - 70 S BUDEAUX Rest Camp - Regt would march under C.O.	Ref QMG 2. E253. Aug 24 G '15
Aug 27th '15 Same place		
Aug 28th '15 Same place	5.15 pm Br. Col. LONG. O.D. representing W.O. Inspected all personnel - accompanied by Lt Col. LANE. A.H. A.D.V.S. inspected the horses of this unit at the Reg'tl Horselines.	
Aug 29 '15 Same place	Nil	
Aug 30th '15 Same place	N.C.	
Aug 31st '15 Same place	2.1st Stop for Minta. Tr Parade. Pvt 10 Rupert Froones Ris Reg'. per 401. The Coming Ref. Sec'y 4 674 Read to Unit.	

Forms/C.2118/11.

DIV TRAIN

General Staff.
60 (London) Division.

Herewith War Diaries of the unit under my command. During the month nearly all available transport has been employed daily in the issue of supplies and the transport of hay from farms to the Supply depôt.

The three Brigade companies are now complete with G.S. waggons, and the Head Quarter Company has received 25 out of a total of 59: including curtain waggons they are now also complete.

All available spare time has been occupied in training the drivers to ride and drive, in which they have made rapid progress toward efficiency.

B.H. Walbrieff.
O.C. A.S.C.
60 (London) Divⁿ

D/534

Bishops Stortford.
8. Sep. 1915

No 2

WAR DIARY or INTELLIGENCE SUMMARY

Army Form C. 2118

(Erase heading not required.)

Instructions regarding War Diaries and Intelligence Summaries are contained in F. S. Regs., Part II and the Staff Manual respectively. Title Pages will be prepared in manuscript.

Place	Date	Hour	Summary of Events and Information	Remarks and references to Appendices
Saffron Walden	10/9/15	12 noon	Inspection by Brigadier ffitch at Littlebury.	
	16/9/15	12 noon	do O.C. A.S.C. do	
	16/9/15	4.30 p.m.	Practice entraining & detraining at Saffron Walden Station	
	13/9/15	4.30 a.m.	Inspection by A.D.S.&T.	
	18/9/15	9.15 a.m.	Inspection by O.C. A.S.C.	
	"	6 p.m.	Practice entraining & detraining.	
	23/9/15	12 noon	Inspection of Composite Brigade by Genl Colby at Greenbox Park	Attached Capt N°2 Co A.S.C.

A.F.C.2148.
ON TRAIN

War Diary.

Hour and Place	Summary of Events and Information	Remarks
9.a.m. 1st September '15 BISHOP'S STORTFORD.	I have to report that during the month of August great improvement is found in Camp accommodation, shower baths have been erected and men are thereby enabled to bathe frequently. Transport work is still being carried out satisfactorily and both men and horses are working well. The Company have now 25 new Wagons and 27 sets of Ride & Drive Harness and the men are being trained in the use of same. I am of opinion that it will be an improvement on the old Harness also in use. As the men are keen on this Harness, I venture to say that they will not be long before they are proficient in the use of same. I have to report that every effort is being made to keep the horses therein in good condition.	

[signature]
CAPTAIN.
CO.
HEADQUARTERS, T.&S.C'L.
LONDON.

War Diary of Intelligence Summary

Hour, Date, Place	Summary of Events & Information	Remarks & references to appendices.
12 Noon. Windmill Camp Bishops Stortford. Sunday 3rd October 1915.	**Training** This is proceeding very satisfactorily. Among other exercises the Company has been practised in entraining on two occasions - the experience then gained was most useful - 4 Wagons (side-loading) and 32 Horses were entrained in 20 minutes & detrained in 12 minutes. This speaks well for the efficiency of the Co. in this respect. Training in actual convoy work has been very heavy owing to the large amount of Hay & Wood required for the Horses of the Division. On Sep. 15. the Co. was called upon to supply Transport for Ammunition to be taken to Qr. Had hm t on a telephone message being received & without any preliminary warning a convoy of 15 Wagons (with full complement of billqueuers) was turned out on the road in 17 minutes. This speaks for the general efficiency of the Company as regards the work of an A.S.C. unit. **Discipline** This is still of a high standard. very few minor offences have had to be dealt with. **Transport Service.** The transport of the Brigade is done by this Co. and also a large proportion for the Divisional Troops as explained under Training above. **Billets & Messing** The whole Co. is still under Canvas & the men are very endured especially with regard to the food. The Generous scale of rations & monetary allowance leaves a good margin for varying the meals & so adds to their comfort & generally keeps them fit & in good health. C. Colon Shieldsun Capt. O.C. 181st Brigade Coy. A.S.C.	

A.F.C.2118.

War Diary

Date. Time. Place	Summary of Events and Information.	References to Remarks & Appx.
9.a.m. 2nd OCTOBER 1915 BISHOP'S STORTFORD	I have to report that during the Month of September the work performed and the training, whenever opportunity availed, was accomplished in a most satisfactory manner by this Company. Entraining and Detraining practice has been carried out successfully, 30 horses and four wagons being entrained in 15 minutes. Harnessing horses and hooking in to wagons in the dark has also been successfully undertaken, the average time being 10 to 12 minutes from the Stables which are about 400 yards away from the Wagon Park. The Transport work during the month has been very heavy, large convoys being required for Ammunition and fetching Hay and Wood from out lying Farms in addition to the ordinary daily supply work. The majority of the men are getting skilled in Ride and Drive and a great deal of the spare time has to be taken up in cleaning Harness. Great credit is due to the N.C.O's and Men for the excellent and willing manner in which the work has been done. The horses are in good condition and there is a very small percentage of sick horses. F.K.Luy CAPTAIN. HEADQUARTERS COMPANY. 60th (LONDON) DIVISIONAL TRAIN.	

DIN TRAIN ①

Army Form C. 2118.

WAR DIARY
or
INTELLIGENCE SUMMARY.
(Erase heading not required.)

Instructions regarding War Diaries and Intelligence Summaries are contained in F.S. Regs., Part II. and the Staff Manual respectively. Title pages will be prepared in manuscript.

Hour, Date, Place	Summary of Events and Information	Remarks and references to Appendices
Saffron Walden 5 Oct/15	The Company took part in a Divisional Tactical Exercise from the 5th to the 8th inst. inclusive. The first night the Company bivouacked at Potting, the second night at Braintree, & the third at Potting, returning from there to camp at Saffron Walden on the fourth day.	
Saffron Walden 13 Oct/15	The Company took part in a further Divisional Tactical Exercise on the 11th & 12th. On the 11th it with the Baggage & Supplies of the Brigade to Great Pelham, where it bivouacked for the night, returning to camp the next day. Captain Howard, O.C. No 2 Coy left for France.	
Saffron Walden 16 Oct/15		
Saffron Walden 22 Oct/15	On the 19th, 20th, 21st & 22nd the Company took part in a repetition of the first Divisional Tactical Exercise. On this occasion the transport was carried by the Supply Column being detached from _____	

Forms/C. 2118/10

(9 29 6) W 4141—463 100,000 9/14 H W V Forms/C. 2118/10

(2) Final

Army Form C. 2118.

WAR DIARY
or
INTELLIGENCE SUMMARY
(Erase heading not required.)

Hour, Date, Place	Summary of Events and Information	Remarks and references to Appendices
Bishop's Stortford. 27 Oct/15	The rest of the company & dismounting NCOs arrived on the night of the 24th. From there they proceeded to Loughing Pont- Good junction N of White Notley, & stayed to harness the same day. On the 24th Sgt White Cochrane sent 12 repairs to assist in the move of the 180th Infantry Brigade from Nuffield Broad Oak to Gaston Hadham. This was carried out the following day. On the 26th & 27th October the 174th & 176th Infantry Brigade moved from Gaston Hadham to Bishop's Stortford. The company was employed in helping these moves. The whole convoy was inspected while on the road by General Langton. On this day Lt. Tomkins rejoined for duty from No 3 Coy. B.S.Campbell 2/Lt ASC Capt 179th Infantry Brigade Train Coy.	

Forms/C. 2118/10

WAR DIARY
or
INTELLIGENCE SUMMARY. Sept?
(Erase heading not required.)

Army Form C. 2118.

Hour, Date, Place	Summary of Events and Information	Remarks and references to Appendices
2nd October 1916. Fairfield Broad Oak Essex.	The Month has passed without anything of unusual importance having occurred. This Company has had a large amount of Transport Work to perform, owing to the Battalions in the Brigade having been ordered to hand over all their Waggons to the R.F.A. The execution of this Transport Work has been greatly impeded by the want to this Company	

Army Form C. 2118.

WAR DIARY
or
INTELLIGENCE SUMMARY.
(Erase heading not required.)

Instructions regarding War Diaries and Intelligence Summaries are contained in F.S. Regs., Part II. and the Staff Manual respectively. Title pages will be prepared in manuscript.

Hour, Date, Place	Summary of Events and Information	Remarks and references to Appendices
2nd October, 1915. Fobfield, Brentwood, Essex.	at 2 AM Barn Waggons, which are totally unsuited for our work. The horses have arrived with a few exceptions kept in good condition. The health of the Troops has been excellent. Discipline has been good. Training has progressed satisfactorily. T.F. Lay Capt. 160th Infantry Brigade 1st ASC	

WAR DIARY
or
INTELLIGENCE SUMMARY.
(Erase heading not required.)

Army Form C. 2118.

Hour, Date, Place	Summary of Events and Information	Remarks and references to Appendices
Littlebury Essex 31st Oct. 1916.	During the past Month this Company has had a large amount of Work to perform. Transport work has been Heavy. Tactical Exercises were performed on the 8th, to the 8th instant inclusive again on the 14th, 14th & 15th instant I personally was not present upon either Occasion owing to indisposition. It was reported to me however that the men & horses carried out their Part of the work quite satisfactorily. On the 19th instant we again	

Army Form C. 2118.

WAR DIARY
or
INTELLIGENCE SUMMARY.
(Erase heading not required.)

Hour, Date, Place	Summary of Events and Information	Remarks and references to Appendices
Lippitts ? Essex 31st Oct. 1915.	Performed 4 days Tactical Exercise. I was very pleased with the way this Company carried out its feats which was at times very strenuous. On the 23rd instant we with the assistance of the other Companies moved the 110th Infantry Brigade from "Fairfields" Broad Oak Camp, to Saffron Walden. On the following day the 26th instant we moved the 179th Infantry Brigade to Bishops Stortford. We were inspected on the road	

Army Form C. 2118.

WAR DIARY
or
INTELLIGENCE SUMMARY.

(Erase heading not required.)

Instructions regarding War Diaries and Intelligence Summaries are contained in F.S. Regs., Part II. and the Staff Manual respectively. Title pages will be prepared in manuscript.

Hour, Date, Place	Summary of Events and Information	Remarks and references to Appendices
Lillebury Essex. 31st Oct. 1915.	"General Inspection" by General ~~~~~~ who had but few faults to find. On the 28th inst. Colonel Long inspected my horses & expressed himself as pleased with their condition. The health of the troops under my Command has been good & there has been no crime. N.F. Day Capt.	

[Stamp: 180th INFANTRY BRIGADE COMPANY * NIVRI * ……… DIV. TRAIN]

DIV TRAIN

Head Quarters.
60 (London) Division.

I have the honour to attach herewith, War Diaries of the Unit under my command. During the month the usual transport and supply work have been satisfactorily carried on. One Officer and 28 NCOs and men have been detached to the Transport School at Shoreham; one Officer has proceeded overseas to join the First Line Unit, and four Officers have been placed under orders to proceed. A medical board has found one Officer unfit for service and two Officers fit only for home service: I have so far received no directions as to the disposal of these Officers.

B. D. Melrose Col.
O.C. A.S.C. 60 (London) Division

D/933

Bishops Stortford.
5 Oct. 1915.

Head Quarters.
60 (London) Division.

Attached please find War Diaries of the Unit under my command.

The work has been heavy during the month. From the 5 to the 8 Oct. and from the 19th to the 22nd; the whole of the vehicles were employed in Divisional Tactical Exercises in the neighbourhood of Braintree. The whole of the work was satisfactorily performed and the horses stood the work well. One horse died during the operations on the 6 October, from Colic: a board has been held and the proceedings forwarded to the A.D.V.S.

During the fortnight commencing 25 Oct; the whole of the vehicles were employed in moving the various units of the Division in change of station: this work was satisfactorily performed without any casualty.

On the 26 October, Major General London, inspected the various companies, and a convoy of 90 wagons on the march from Saffron Walden to Bishops Stortford.

The condition of the horses is good, and the health and conduct of the men leaves nothing to be desired.

B.P. Dalbiac Col.
O.C. A.S.C. 60 (London) Division.

6/409.
Bishops Stortford.
5 Nov. 1915.

WAR DIARY
or
INTELLIGENCE SUMMARY
(Erase heading not required.)

Army Form C. 2118

Place	Date	Hour	Summary of Events and Information	Remarks and references to Appendices
Bishops Stortford	1 Nov.	Noon.	The Company furnished a convoy of 16 wagons to assist in the move of portion of 181st Brigade from BISHOPS STORTFORD to BRAINTREE. The convoy was loaded with baggage & stores of the 2/23rd Batt: London Regt. The convoy left HOCKERILL CAMP at 9.30. It took 1 hour & 20 minutes to water & feed at DUNMOW, & arrived at BRAINTREE at 6.15 P.M. As it was then too dark to unload the wagons, they were parked on the parade ground of the 2/23rd Batt, the horses were picketed out & the men billetted with N°4 Coy. Rain fell for the greater portion of the day until the evening.	BHR BHR BHR
"		Weather Road	The road traversed being a main Roman one, the state of the weather did not greatly affect BHR	
"	2 Nov.	Noon.	The convoy returned from BRAINTREE to BISHOPS STORTFORD, halting to water & feed at DUNMOW. BHR	BHR
		Weather	Fine.	
"	4 Nov.	Noon.	The Company furnished 12 wagons to assist in the move of the remainder of the 181st Brigade, namely the 2/23rd and the 2/24th. The convoy proceeded to BRAINTREE as before, leaving HOCKERILL CAMP at 9 A.M. & arriving at about 5 P.M. The men were as before, billetted by Nº4 Coy for the night.	BHR
				Free

WAR DIARY
or
INTELLIGENCE SUMMARY.
(Erase heading not required.)

Army Form C. 2118.

Hour, Date, Place	Summary of Events and Information	Remarks and references to Appendices
3rd Nov. 1915. 12 noon. Drill Hall Victoria Street Braintree Essex.	**Training** Owing to the great amount of Transport Duties performed by this Co. there has been little time for drill, but this has in no way affected the training of the men, as they have been doing their real work. These have been two Divisional Exercises in which the men have performed their duties in a most satisfactory manner. It was found on the first Exercise that it was most essential to keep the Baggage & Supply Trains separate. This idea being acted upon on the Second Exercise everything went well. It was also found that it was advisable to keep the Hd Qrs of the Co. near Railhead so that an early delivery of Ration could be made to the Units and also so that the Wagons could return & bank up and in personal observation & supervision. One thing that impressed one was the fact that it is possible for a Convoy of 50 Wagons (Horse) to arrive at a given point at the exact moment provided they are properly looked after by Officers of each branch. It is most essential that Convoys are halted and looked over every 5 minutes in each hour. If this is done it is quite possible to do a journey of 35 miles a day without the horses being in any way distressed as was proved on the change of Station from R. Stanford here. **Wirecutting** This continues as one expects **Transport Duties** This is covered by above remarks **Billeting & Hutting** The men are settling down very well in Billets after the open air life and appreciate the comfort of same.	

C. Calor Smallwood Capt.
O.C. 151st Brigade Coy. A.S.C.

WAR DIARY
or
INTELLIGENCE SUMMARY

(Erase heading not required.)

Army Form C. 2118

Instructions regarding War Diaries and Intelligence Summaries are contained in F. S. Regs., Part II. and the Staff Manual respectively. Title Pages will be prepared in manuscript.

Place	Date	Hour	Summary of Events and Information	Remarks and references to Appendices
Bishops Stortford	4 Nov		As on 1st Nov.	PSR
"	5 Nov		Abstr 52. Fine.	PSR
"			Marc. The convoy should supply to BISHOPS STORTFORD supplying to water & fill at DUNMOW.	PSR
"			Abstr 52. Heavy rain.	PSR
"	11 Nov		Convoy Coy RE HQ 66 coys to the AD.V.P. & extract at troops at Bishops Stortford.	PSR
"	12 Nov		Marc. The outposts furnished a convoy of 10 wagons of the 2nd coys of Bn to some of Elsenham Hall. The convoy left at-HAM, leaving station from BISHOPS STORTFORD to ELSENHAM returning at 5 PM.	PSR
"			Roads. Moderate. Conveying & harbors on approaching ELSENHAM.	PSR
"			Abstr 52. Fine.	PSR
"	17 Nov		Transfer. From GHQ HD 15 hampshire to 2/15 GHQ RFA.	PSR
"	19 Nov		Abstr 52. Bay Rgd HD transferred to 1st Case HRm hospital R.Albans this is transfer to this unit as from this date.	PSR

1875 Wt. W 593/826 1,000,000 4/15 J.B.C. & A. A.D.S.S./Forms/C. 2118.

Army Form C. 2118

WAR DIARY
or
INTELLIGENCE SUMMARY
(Erase heading not required.)

Instructions regarding War Diaries and Intelligence Summaries are contained in F.S. Regs., Part II and the Staff Manual respectively. Title Pages will be prepared in manuscript.

Place	Date	Hour	Summary of Events and Information	Remarks and references to Appendices
Bishops Stortford	26 Nov.	Strength	Capt R. Pearson having absorbed into 1st Line is struck off this strength from 3rd Nov. Capt B. Van Someren posted to HQrs Coy from 23rd Nov.	Corps Order No 313. 24 Nov/15 B.S.R.
"	27 "	Casualty	Pay Sgt G. Piper no. 01007 6/ D.A.P.S. struck off strength.	B.S.R.
"	28 "	"	Sent to 1st Home Counties F.A. by Hospital 8 officers, since struck off strength B.S.R.	B.S.R.
"	29 "	Move	The company furnished a convoy of 8 lorries to convoy 2/6 Hunts Rgt from BISHOPS STORTFORD to WARE. The lorries moved at 10.30 AM & numbered by way of MUCH HADHAM, where the convoy halted for 1 hour & 30 minutes to water & feed, WIDFORD, WARESIDE, to WARE, arriving at 3.30 PM. Lorries & men were billeted for the night in WARE, rations being taken.	B.S.R.
"	"	Bombs	The men taken were kilts & in khaki aprons, weather fair.	B.S.R.
"	"	Weather	In light rain throughout the day.	
"	30 "	Move	The convoy returned to BISHOPS STORTFORD by the same route.	B.S.R.
"	"	Weather	Fine.	B.S.R.

B.S. Trowell Capt
179th Infantry Brigade Train Coy.

Army Form C. 2118.

WAR DIARY
or
INTELLIGENCE SUMMARY.
(Erase heading not required.)

Hour, Date, Place	Summary of Events and Information	Remarks and references to Appendices
1st November 1915 Finchley Essex.	N.f. Nothing of note	
2nd Nov.	N.f. Twelve waggons sent to Bishops Stortford to assist in moving 189th Brigade to Braintree.	
3rd Nov	N.f. Nothing of note	
4th "	N.f. Nothing of note	
5th Nov.	N.f. 12 Waggons from No 2 Coy moved remainder of 179th Brigade to Bishops Stortford.	
6th Nov.	N.f. 12 Waggons returned from Braintree. No casualties	

Army Form C. 2118.

WAR DIARY
or
INTELLIGENCE SUMMARY.
(Erase heading not required.)

Instructions regarding War Diaries and Intelligence Summaries are contained in F.S. Regs., Part II. and the Staff Manual respectively. Title pages will be prepared in manuscript.

2.

Hour, Date, Place	Summary of Events and Information	Remarks and references to Appendices
7th Nov	Nothing of note	
8th Nov	Nothing of note	
9th Nov	Nothing of note	
10th Nov	Nothing of note	
	Dr Atkinson Junr took up duties as R.M.O.	
11th Nov	14 Horses issued from sick lines	
12th Nov	10 Mules received from R.F.A. for Brigade Headquarters.	
13th Nov	Nothing of note	

Army Form C. 2118.

WAR DIARY
or
INTELLIGENCE SUMMARY.

(Erase heading not required.)

Instructions regarding War Diaries and Intelligence
Summaries are contained in F.S. Regs., Part II.
and the Staff Manual respectively. Title pages
will be prepared in manuscript.

Hour, Date, Place	Summary of Events and Information	Remarks and references to Appendices
14th Nov	wt.f. Nothing of Note	
15th Nov	" "	
16th Nov	" "	
17th Nov	" "	
18th Nov	" "	
19th Nov	" "	
20th Nov	" "	
21st Nov	wt.f. Inspection of Billets by 3rd 2nd Army Major Fegan + Brigade..	

Army Form C. 2118.

WAR DIARY
or
INTELLIGENCE SUMMARY.
(Erase heading not required.)

Instructions regarding War Diaries and Intelligence Summaries are contained in F. S. Regs., Part II and the Staff Manual respectively. Title pages will be prepared in manuscript.

Hour, Date, Place	Summary of Events and Information	Remarks and references to Appendices
22nd Nov	Nothing of note	
23rd Nov	Lieut. Fletcher from 71st Column reported for duty.	
24th Nov	Inoculations commenced	
25th Nov	Inspected by Colonel Dalbrac	
26th Nov	Nothing of note	
27th Nov	" "	
28th Nov	" "	
29th Nov	" "	
30th Nov	" "	

Army Form C. 2118.

WAR DIARY
or
INTELLIGENCE SUMMARY.
(Erase heading not required.)

Instructions regarding War Diaries and Intelligence Summaries are contained in F.S. Regs., Part II and the Staff Manual respectively. Title pages will be prepared in manuscript.

Hour, Date, Place	Summary of Events and Information	Remarks and references to Appendices

General. N.f. The health of the Troops has been excellent.

No Crime.

Horses in good condition.

Training Progressing satisfactorily.

Billeted with subsistance from the 11th Nov. 1915.

W.H. Jay. Capt.
No. 3. Coy. A.S.C.
30th Nov. 1915.

A.F.C. 2118.

WAR DIARY of the HEADQUARTERS COMPANY (60th Divisional Train)

Date, Time, Place.	Summary of Events and Information.	Remarks & References to Appendices.
Nov. 1st, 1915. 9 a.m. BISHOPS STORTFORD.	I have to report that for the month of October very excellent work has been performed by this Company. Headquarters Company carried out their duties during the Manoeuvres in a satisfactory manner, and the experience gained will be beneficial to the men. My Company have also assisted in the removal of troops of the Division, and the Transport was accomplished satisfactorily. The N.C.O's and men have worked well, and all duties performed in an efficient manner. Heavy transport work is still being carried out by the Company and the work is being performed without a hitch. The Horses have worked well, but owing to the strain placed upon them by Manoeuvres and Moves and also the usual Transport Work, a number have gone sick. Taking into consideration the very heavy work which is being carried out, I am of opinion that the Horses are in good condition and the percentage of sick is reasonable. All the drivers are efficient in driving and the practical experience gained this month should prove of great benefit. A large amount of fatigue would be spared the horses should it be Long Rein driving.	

[signature]
Lieutenant,
Headquarters Company,
60th (London) Divisional Train.

Army Form C. 2118.

WAR DIARY
~~INTELLIGENCE~~ SUMMARY.
(Erase heading not required.)

Instructions regarding War Diaries and Intelligence Summaries are contained in F.S. Regs., Part II. and the Staff Manual respectively. Title pages will be prepared in manuscript.

Hour, Date, Place	Summary of Events and Information	Remarks and references to Appendices
BISHOP'S STORTFORD		
16/10/15	Major A.J. MAURICE joined from Overseas.	A.A.
19/10/15	" Left on weeks leave.	A.A.
24/10/15	" rejoined.	A.A.
28/10/15	Horse inspection.	A.A.
29/10/15	Convoy for 2/15 Bn. Co. of Hon. Regt. of 40 wagons out of 25, on their move to WARE. Party billeted there for the night 29-30/10/15.	A.A.
	Convoys for Supplies daily, except Sundays.	A.A.

J. Maurice Major
Comdg H.S.Co. 60. Divn

Army Form C. 2118.

WAR DIARY
or
INTELLIGENCE SUMMARY.

(Erase heading not required.)

Instructions regarding War Diaries and Intelligence Summaries are contained in F.S. Regs., Part II. and the Staff Manual respectively. Title pages will be prepared in manuscript.

Hour, Date, Place	Summary of Events and Information	Remarks and references to Appendices
Braintree, Essex. 12. noon. 2nd December 1915.	Training. This has been entirely covered by the ordinary A.S.C Duties. Transport of Supplies to outlying Battalion at Coggeshall & Dunmow and Convoys for Hay & Straw daily, together with delivery of Supplies in the town to the Units there have occupied the attention of all the men for each day. This has provided much actual drill done; however the men are thoroughly trained in their duties in every branch. Entraining was carried out both by light and dark on Sunday last the 28th inst. and was most satisfactory in every way. CCl. Discipline. This is exemplary. CCl. Transport Duties. The 21st Battalion being at Coggeshall and the 2nd Dunmow and having to be rationed, it has been found advisable to allow the train doing these journeys to be worked in rotation so that they came in every third day. This has worked very well so far. CCl. Billeting Mustering. The men are billeted close at hand but unfortunately the horses are rather scattered and this adds to the work and takes up considerable time. The men billets are very comfortable ones in private houses. CCl.	

C. Calvin Fuller
Capt.
O.C. 181st Brigade Coy. A.S.C.

Confidential

War Diary of
180th Infantry Brigade No 1186

from 1st December 1915 to 31st December 1915

VOLUME 2. No. 12

No. 3 Coy.

WAR DIARY 60th Ldn. Divisional Train. Army Form C. 2118.

INTELLIGENCE SUMMARY.

(Erase heading not required.)

Instructions regarding War Diaries and Intelligence Summaries are contained in F.S. Regs., Part II. and the Staff Manual respectively. Title pages will be prepared in manuscript.

Hour, Date, Place	Summary of Events and Information	Remarks and references to Appendices
1.12.15. Littlebury.	Colonel LANE. A.D.V.S. Inspected Food & cook Two: none available heavy enough to exchange the horses in charge too small for our work.	W.F.J.
2.12.15 "	Move of 2/20th Battalion to HAVERHILL. Motored to HAVERHILL in afternoon and fixed "CROWN INN" HEMPSTEAD for Refilling Point.	W.F.J.
3.12.15 "	Refilling Point satisfactory Convoy returned 3.P.M.	W.F.J.
4.12.15 "	Company Training & Transport Work	W.F.J.
5.12.15 "	Training Practice at SAFFRON WALDEN	W.F.J.

No 3. Coy

WAR DIARY 60th Ldn. Divisional Train. Army Form C. 2118.

INTELLIGENCE SUMMARY

(Erase heading not required.)

Hour, Date, Place	Summary of Events and Information	Remarks and references to Appendices
5.12.15. Littlebury	This was carried out satisfactorily	W.F.J.
6.12.15. "	Transport Work & Company Training	W.F.J.
7.12.15. "	Transport Work & Company Training. 2. Horses sold. SAFFRON WALDEN.	W.F.J.
8.12.15. "	Dr Burrows 2/18 th London Regiment reported as M.O. to this Company for the first time. Went to Headquarters Bishops Stortford in afternoon	W.F.J.
9.12.15 "	Went Bishops Stortford detached 10.H.D Horses 1. Rider	W.F.J.
10.12.15. "	Transport work. Inspected 2/18th Transport sent two horses V. Hospital.	W.F.J.

Army Form C. 2118.

WAR DIARY of 60th Lan. Divisional Train.

No. 3 Coy.

INTELLIGENCE SUMMARY.

(Erase heading not required.)

Instructions regarding War Diaries and Intelligence Summaries are contained in F. S. Regs., Part II and the Staff Manual respectively. Title pages will be prepared in manuscript.

Hour, Date, Place	Summary of Events and Information	Remarks and references to Appendices
11.12.15 Littlebury	Transport Duties. Company Training.	W.S.J.
12.12.15 "	Inspection of Stables & Harness	W.S.J.
13.12.15 "	Transport Work. Company Training.	W.S.J.
14.12.15 "	" "	W.S.J.
15.12.15 "	Transport Work. Inspection of Transport at SAFFRON WALDEN postponed owing to Rain.	W.S.J.
16.12.15 "	Company Training & Transport.	W.S.J.
17.12.15 "	Transport Duties. Inspection of Battalion Transport Personnel. Riding School.	W.S.J.

Army Form C. 2118.

WAR DIARY
60 (Eden Divisional Train.
No 3. Coy.
INTELLIGENCE SUMMARY.

(Erase heading not required.)

Instructions regarding War Diaries and Intelligence Summaries are contained in F.S. Regs., Part II. and the Staff Manual respectively. Title pages will be prepared in manuscript.

Hour, Date, Place	Summary of Events and Information	Remarks and references to Appendices
18.12.15. Littlebury	Transport duties. Company Training.	W.F.
19.12.15. "	Inspection of all Horses Hoofes & Harness. Lieut Fletcher away on week-end leave.	W.F.
20.12.15. "	Transport duties. Made arrangements with R.A.M.C. to take over Transport on the 22nd Dec. 1915.	W.F.
21.12.15. "	Transport duties Lieut Fletcher away on Board at Bishops Stortford. Orders received from Brigade Headquarters re Inspection by G.O.C. on 22nd Dec.	W.F.

WAR DIARY of No.3 Coy. 60th Ldn. Divisional Train. Army Form C. 2118.

INTELLIGENCE SUMMARY.

(Erase heading not required.)

Instructions regarding War Diaries and Intelligence Summaries are contained in F.S. Regs., Part II. and the Staff Manual respectively. Title pages will be prepared in manuscript.

Hour, Date, Place	Summary of Events and Information	Remarks and references to Appendices
22.12.15. Tilbury.	Inspection by G.O.C. 12.45.P.M. at SAFFRON WALDEN. Paraded all available wagons spare horses Brigade Mules and Men.	W.F.J.
23.12.15 "	Took over R.A.M.C. Transport Section, Transport Duties Company Training.	W.F.J.
24.12.15 "	Company Training. To Transport.	W.F.J.
25.12.15: "	Christmas Day away on leave.	"
26.12.15 "	Inspection of all stables horses and Harness.	W.F.J.
27.12.15 "	Transport with D.A.D.O.S. called & inspected Shoes.	W.F.J.

No. 3. Coy. WAR DIARY 60th Lond. Divisional Train. Army Form C. 2118.

INTELLIGENCE SUMMARY.
(Erase heading not required.)

Hour, Date, Place	Summary of Events and Information	Remarks and references to Appendices
28.12.15. Littlebury.	Inspected all horses of Brigade preparatory to Col LANE's Inspection for Cas. Comp. on the 29th Dec. 1915.	W.F.J.
29.12.15 "	Transport duties. Col. LANE. A.D.V.S. Cas. 5 horses. 3 to go to V. Hospital St ALBANS. 3 to be transferred.	W.F.J.
30.12.15 "	On Board the Bishops Stortford re Letter Book & accidents to horses.	W.F.J.
31.12.15 "	Transport duties. On Board re deaths of horses 2/18th Battalion	W.F.J.

W.F.J. Jay
Capt
No. 3. Coy. 60th London Divisional Train.

CONFIDENTIAL.

WAR DIARY OF

179th Infantry Brigade Train Company.

From 1st December 1915 to the 31st December. 1915.

VOLUME 2. No. 12.

Army Form C. 2118

WAR DIARY
INTELLIGENCE SUMMARY
(Erase heading not required.)

Instructions regarding War Diaries and Intelligence Summaries are contained in F. S. Regs., Part II. and the Staff Manual respectively. Title Pages will be prepared in manuscript.

Place	Date	Hour	Summary of Events and Information	Remarks and references to Appendices
Bishop's Stortford	20.12.15	3.30 pm	Company work. G.O.C. 60th LONDON DIVISION inspected transport of this Company.	Appendix "A"
"	21.12.15		Company work.	Do.
"	22.12.15		Company work.	Do.
"	23.12.15		Company work.	Do.
"	24.12.15		Company work. Huts erected for Wheelers, Farriers, Quarter-Master Stores and Forage nearly completed and inhabited on this day.	Do.
"	25.12.15	6.30 pm	Christmas dinner for all ranks of this Company. Stable routine.	Do.
"	26.12.15		Company work. Church Parade.	Do.
"	27.12.15		Stable routine.	Do.
"	28.12.15		Lieut RANDALL returned from ALDERSHOT and assumed command.	Do.
"	29.12.15		Company work.	Do.
"	30.12.15		Company training. Company and Transport O.R.	
"	31.12.15		Company training. Transport O.R.	

B.E. Randall Lieut
O/C 1/60th Infantry Brigade Train

WAR DIARY or INTELLIGENCE SUMMARY

Army Form C. 2118

(Erase heading not required.)

Place	Date	Hour	Summary of Events and Information	Remarks and references to Appendices
Bishops Stortford	1.12.15		Convoy work.	Sto.
	2.12.15	2.15 p.m.	D.A.D.O.S. condemned cast clothing and inspected clothing of every man in the Company. He sanctioned new issues in some cases.	Sto.
	3.12.15		Convoy work. 1 horse sold	Sto.
	4.12.15		Convoy work. 2 Riding horses received from Headquarters Company.	Sto.
	5.12.15		Horses cleaning and stable routine	Sto.
	6.12.15		Convoy work.	Sto.
	7.12.15		Convoy work. Lieut RANDALL proceeded to ALDERSHOT for a course of instruction and Lieut WORNUM assumed command.	Sto.
	8.12.15		Convoy work	Sto.
	9.12.15		Convoy work. 10 horses received from Headquarters Company.	Sto.
	10.12.15	11.45 a.m.	Convoy work. Brigadier-General W. B. BROWN with the D.D.R.E. inspected the horses of work performed in road making in the Camp and the site of the proposed Wagon Park which is to be covered into clinker.	Sto.
	11.12.15		Convoy work.	Sto.
	12.12.15		Horses cleaning and stable routine	Sto.
	13.12.15		Convoy work	Sto.
	14.12.15		Convoy work	Sto.
	15.12.15		Convoy work	Sto.
	16.12.15		Convoy work. 10 mules received from Headquarters 179th Infantry Brigade. 8 horses sold.	Sto.
	17.12.15	2.15 p.m.	Convoy work. Small kit inspection	Sto.
	"	2.45 p.m.	Brigadier-General T.P.C. OMLEY visited the Camp.	Sto.
	18.12.15		Convoy work	Sto.
	19.12.15		Horses cleaning and stable routine	Sto.

APPENDIX 'A'

Inspection by G.O.C. 60th London Division

The G.O.C 60th London Division inspected the transport of this Company in marching order in column of route at 3.30pm. Monday 20th December. 1915 at WARWICK ROAD. BISHOPS. STORTFORD.

There were 3 Officers, 65 other ranks. 38 horses and 14 wagons present at this inspection.

CONFIDENTIAL.

War Diary of No: 4 Company A.S.C.
60th (London) Divisional Train

From 1st December 1915 to the 31st December 1915.

VOLUME 2. No: 12.

Confidential

WAR DIARY of 19th Brigade Co. A.S.C. Army Form C. 2118.

INTELLIGENCE SUMMARY. From 1st December 1915 to 31st December 1915

(Erase heading not required.)

Instructions regarding War Diaries and Intelligence Summaries are contained in F. S. Regs., Part II. and the Staff Manual respectively. Title pages will be prepared in manuscript.

Hour, Date, Place	Summary of Events and Information	Remarks and references to Appendices
1.12.15. Braintree	Convoys for Brigade Supplies to & for Company Orders.	C.O.J.
2.12.15. Do.	Captain C.C. Swallow attended a Board at Bishops Stortford in reference to handing over H.Q. Co. to Major Maurice.	C.O.J.
3.12.15. Do.	Convoys for Brigade Supplies & Do.	C.O.J.
4.12.15. Do.	Convoys for Brigade Supplies to Do. (Double Issue) R.A.M.C. Evac. Hospital transfers	C.O.J.
5.12.15. Do.	Harness cleaning & Inspection by O.C.	C.O.J.
6.12.15. Do.	Convoys for Brigade Supplies to	C.O.J.
7.12.15. Do.	Capt Swallow attended Court of Enquiry at Braintree to Enquire into the loss of certain Arms & Ammunition. Convoy for Brigade Supplies to	C.O.J.
8.12.15. Do.	Convoys for Brigade Supplies to. Capt Swallow attend Brig. HQ. re Computer Supplies.	C.O.J.
9.12.15. Do.	Capt Wellington & Lieut St Burns & Redwood attended Board at Hull	C.O.J.
	Hull Braintree to Enquire into damage to G.S. Wagon.	C.O.J.
10.12.15. Do.	Convoys for Brigade Supplies to (Double Issue)	C.O.J.
11.12.15. Do.	Convoys for Brigade Supplies to	C.O.J.
12.12.15. Do.	Harness Cleaning & Inspection by O.C. of all horses both Draught and Riders fully harnessed & saddled to ascertain if all harness complete & in good condition. Very satisfactory except in two cases this was rectified in the afternoon by these Drivers.	C.O.J.

Army Form C. 2118.

WAR DIARY
of
INTELLIGENCE SUMMARY.
(Erase heading not required.)

Instructions regarding War Diaries and Intelligence Summaries are contained in F. S. Regs., Part II. and the Staff Manual respectively. Title pages will be prepared in manuscript.

Hour, Date, Place	Summary of Events and Information	Remarks and references to Appendices
13.12.15. Braintree.	Convoys for Brigade Supplies to a/per Company Orders	ccs.
14.12.15. Do.	Do.	ccs.
15.12.15. Do.	Do.	ccs.
16.12.15. Do.	Do. O.C. Dist. Train inspected 2/6. T. Ambulance Transport handed on to this Brigade Co.	ccs.
17.12.15. Do.	Do.	ccs.
18.12.15. Do.	Do.	ccs.
19.12.15. Do.	Harness cleaning & inspection by O.C. at 11.0. A.M. Result very satisfactory	ccs.
20.12.15. Do.	Capt. Smallwood attended Board at Rickl(?)s Stanford to enquire into loss to a/per Par 3 of Div. Ordr. No. 3+7. of 10/12/15. Convoys for Brigade Supplies to a/per Company Orders. Capt. Whittington attended Board at Brigade H.Q. Braintree to enquire into the quality of hay. 2nd Lieut Bruno attended a Meeting of the Buttering Committee at Brigade H.Q. Braintree.	
21.12.15. Do.	Convoy for Brigade Supplies & Inspection of Rifles by M.O.	ccs.
22.12.15. Do.	Do.	ccs.
23.12.15. Do.	Usual Convoys as far as possible in morning. Remainder completed in afternoon owing to Inspection by G.O.C. He expressed great satisfaction with the turn-out.	ccs.

Army Form C. 2118.

WAR DIARY

INTELLIGENCE SUMMARY.
(Erase heading not required.)

Instructions regarding War Diaries and Intelligence
Summaries are contained in F.S. Regs., Part II.
and the Staff Manual respectively. Title pages
will be prepared in manuscript.

Hour, Date, Place	Summary of Events and Information	Remarks and references to Appendices
24.12.15 Pracukel	Usual Convoys for Brigade Supplies, Hay etc. Extra heavy work owing to Xmas.	C.C.S.
25.12.15 D⁰	Christmas Day. New release of all possible duties except Stables. Xmas Dinner given by Officers of Co. Same very much enjoyed by N.C.Os & men. all Officers of Company present.	C.C.S.
26.12.15 D⁰	Convoys for Brigade Supplies &c. Capt. Smallwood proceeded on leave.	C.C.S.
27.12.15 D⁰	Moving Day. General Holiday.	C.C.S.
28.12.15 D⁰	Convoy for Brigade Supplies. Capt. Smallwood returned from leave & proceeded to Bishop Stortford to continue Board on per Bde. Order N⁰ 347.	C.C.S.
29.12.15 D⁰	Convoys for Brigade Supplies. Capt. Smallwood returned from Board.	C.C.S.
30.12.15 D⁰	Attended Brigade Exercise in charge of 2nd Line Train, but has none of our wagons out owing to heavy Convoys &c today. 10 Wagons for Hay to Huddersfield.	C.C.S.
31.12.15 D⁰	Convoys for Brigade Supplies &c. O.C. inspected Billets, Messing arrangement Stables &c.	C.C.S.

C. Calver Smallwood
Capt.
O.C. 181st Brigade Coy. A.S.C.

Confidential.

War Diary of

Headquarters Company, 60th (Lond.) Div¹ Train.

from 1st Decr. to 31st Decr., 1915.

VOLUME 2. No: 12

WAR DIARY of H.Q.C. 60th Div. Trans. Army Form C. 2118.

INTELLIGENCE SUMMARY.

(Erase heading not required.)

Page 1.

Instructions regarding War Diaries and Intelligence Summaries are contained in F.S. Regs., Part II. and the Staff Manual respectively. Title pages will be prepared in manuscript.

Hour, Date, Place	Summary of Events and Information	Remarks and references to Appendices
2/12/15 Bishops Stortford	SADDLER DAVIES, 1104, returned to unit after instruction.	A.W.
4/12/15 "	LIEUT: GIBSON took over Supply Duties Divisional Morph.	A.W.
6/12/15 "	LIEUT: BATTLE transferred from Supply to Transport.	A.W.
9/12/15 "	Horse No. 100 died from Cardiac Collapse	A.W.
8/12/15 "	LIEUT: GRIFFITHS proceeded to ALDERSHOT for Course.	A.W.
	40. H.D. horses received from REMOUNT OFFICER.	A.W.
	Dvrs. FIELD, CARDY, KNIGHT & WILKINS went to GROVE PARK from M.T.Cot.	A.W.
	O.C. 2/4 th Lon.Fd. Amb. appointed M.O. to this unit.	A.W.
9/12/15.	10 H.D. & R. horses issued to No. 2 Co:	A.W.
	10 R.D. & M.R. horses " " No. 3 Co:	A.W.
10/12/15 "	Dvrs. FIELD, CARDY, KNIGHT & WILKINS returned	A.W.
12/12/15 "	O.C. Co: interviewed Mr. H. COX re his complaints to G.O.C.	A.W.
13/12/15 "	Harness inspection. Kit inspection.	A.W.
	Court of Inquiry on absence of 990. Dvr. HENBURY	
	Dvr. Scott released for Munition work	A.W.
14/12/15 "	D.C.M. on Driver BERRY charged with stealing watch	A.W.

WAR DIARY of H.Q.Co. 60th Div. Trans.

Army Form C. 2118.

INTELLIGENCE SUMMARY.

(Erase heading not required.)

Page 2.

Hour, Date, Place	Summary of Events and Information	Remarks and references to Appendices
18/12/15 Bishops Stortford.	Dvr BERRY sentenced to 112 days imprisonment commuted to 112 days Detention.	A.U.
18/12/15 "	Sentence on Dvr. BERRY promulgated.	A.U.
19/12/15 "	Kit inspection by O.C. Co. & V.O.	A.U.
20/12/15 "	Inspection of Co. on parade by G.O.C. 60. Divn.	A.U.
21/12/15 "	Dvr. BERRY sent to DETENTION BARRACKS, CHELMSFORD.	A.U.
" "	1 man injured by accident to manure wagon.	A.U.
22/12/15 "	Dvr RALPH released from DETENTION BARRACKS, STAFFORD. 2/Lt. E.C. MOSS transferred to this Coy from 2/24Bn Lon'. Regt. Horse No. 120 died from Cardiac failure. 2/Lt. E.C. MOSS promoted to Captain vice to this Captaincy. Horse No. 119 destroyed by V.O. Suffering from tetanus Coy.	A.U. A.U. A.U.
24/12/15 "	Lieut: GRIFFITHS returned from ALDERSHOT course.	A.U.
" "	Mens Christmas dinner. O.C. Co. went on leave, 2 p.m.	A.U.
27/12/15 "	O.C. Co. returned from leave.	A.U.

WAR DIARY of H.Q. Co. 60th Div. Train.

Army Form C. 2118.

Page 3

INTELLIGENCE SUMMARY.
(Erase heading not required.)

Hour, Date, Place	Summary of Events and Information	Remarks and references to Appendices
28/12/15. Bishops Stortford	Court of Enquiry on absence of 1798 Dvr Smith & 993 Dvr Waldron.	
	Major Maurice assumed command of Train on departure for France of Col: Dalbiac. C.B.	
29/12/15 " "	Horse No. 15 died from hysteria	A.M.
	Board of Officers assembled to check equipment.	A.M.
30/12/15 " "	11 H.D. 9, 3 R. horses sold. Sum realized 243/-.	
	Board on death of horse No. 119 on 24/12/15.	A.M.
	" " damaged wall at Friends' Meeting House	A.M.
	at Coggeshall on 2/11/15.	A.M.
31/12/15 " "	C.Q.C. lectured to N.C.Os on feeding of Horses.	
	C.S.M. Marriott reduced to Sergeant by order of III Army.	

A Maurice Major
Comdg H.Q. Co. 60th Div. Train

WAR DIARY.
of the
160th Infantry Brigade Train Coy.
From Feb. 1st 1916. to Feb. 29. 1916.

Volume III. No 2.

Army Form C. 2118.

WAR DIARY
or
INTELLIGENCE SUMMARY.
(Erase heading not required.)

Instructions regarding War Diaries and Intelligence Summaries are contained in F.S. Regs., Part II and the Staff Manual respectively. Title pages will be prepared in manuscript.

Hour, Date, Place		Summary of Events and Information	Remarks and references to Appendices
Warminster	1-2-16	Convoy. Company Routine.	
"	2-2-16	Lieut. Fletcher granted sick leave. Lieut. Dorman takes command	
"	3-2-16	Stables & Horses washed with disinfectant. Company routine.	
"	4-2-16	Stables & Horses washed with disinfectant.	
"	5-2-16	Stables & Horses washed with disinfectant. Company Routine. Pay Parade	
"		Lost horse & mule sent to O i/c Remounts, Bishop's Stortford. Convoy &	
"	6-2-16	Company Routine.	
"	7-2-16	Church Parade.	
"	8-2-16	Convoy. Company Routine.	
"	9-2-16	Convoy. Company Routine.	
"	10-2-16	Convoy. Company Routine.	
"	11-2-16	Convoy. Company Routine. Hot baths for all men of Coy.	
"	12-2-16	Convoy. Company Routine. Pay Parade.	
"	13-2-16	Convoy. Company Routine.	
"	14-2-16	Church Parade.	
"		2/Lieut. Charrington is attached to the Company & reported for duty.	
"	15-2-16	Lieut. Watton. A.D.C. inspected all horses in Coy. Convoy & Company Routine	
"	16-2-16	Convoy & Company Routine.	
"		Convoy & Company Routine.	

WAR DIARY
or
INTELLIGENCE SUMMARY.
(Erase heading not required.)

Army Form C. 2118.

Hour, Date, Place		Summary of Events and Information	Remarks and references to Appendices
Warminster	17.2.16.	Convoy. Company routine. Hot baths for all men in Convoy.	do.
"	18.2.16.	Convoy. Company routine. Pay Parade.	do.
"	19.2.16.	Convoy. Company routine.	do.
"	20.2.16.	Church Parade.	do.
"	21.2.16.	Convoy. Company routine. Horses infected b/foot disease	do.
"	22.2.16.	Inspection of all horses of the Company by the Inspector of Remounts	do.
"	23.2.16.	Company routine.	
		Horse clearings which had been suffering from Ringworm for the last three weeks.	
"	2.0 pm 24.2.16	Inspection of Transport by Major-General Landon (C.I.Q.M.G.S.)	see Appx. 'A'
"	7.0 pm. "	Inspection of Company Books etc. by Major-General Landon.	
"	10.30 am "	Instruction by Col Stunes by Captain Blackwell.	
"	11.30 am 24.2.16	Inspection of dressing Room by Captain Blackwell.	
		Convoy. Company Routine.	
"	25.2.16	Convoy. Company Routine. Short lecture for all men of Coy.	
"	26.2.16	Convoy. Company Routine. Pay Parade.	
"	27.2.16	Church Parade.	
"	28.2.16	Convoy. Company routine.	
"	29.2.16	Convoy. Company routine.	

APPENDIX 'A'

Inspection of Transport of this Company by Major-General. F. W. B. Landon. C.B.
(C.I.Q.M.G.S.)

Major-General Landon inspected the transport of this Company on February 23rd 1916 at 2.30 p.m.

2 officers, 29 other ranks, 36 H.D. horses, 10 riders & 18 wagons were on parade.

The wagons were paraded along the BOREHAM ROAD. WARMINSTER.

At 4.45 p.m. Major-General Landon inspected the Stables, Harness Room & huts of the Company & at 7 p.m. he inspected the books & general system of the Company Office.

Army Form C. 2118.

WAR DIARY
or
INTELLIGENCE SUMMARY.

(Erase heading not required.)

Instructions regarding War Diaries and Intelligence Summaries are contained in F.S. Regs., Part II and the Staff Manual respectively. Title pages will be prepared in manuscript.

Hour, Date, Place	Summary of Events and Information	Remarks and references to Appendices
Warminster		
1.2.16	Convoy. Company routine	Sd.
2.2.16	Lieut Fletcher granted sick leave. Lieut Warren takes command. Stables and horses washed with disinfectant. Company routine	Sd.
3.2.16	Stables and horses washed with disinfectant. Hot baths for all men in Company. Horses inspected by Lieut Morton, A.V.C.	Sd.
4.2.16	Stables, men and horses washed with disinfectant. Company routine	Sd.
5.2.16	Pay Parade. Cast horse and mule sent to O/C Remounts, Bishop's Stortford.	Sd.
6.2.16	Convoy. Company routine	Sd.
	Church Parade.	Sd.
7.2.16	Convoy. Company routine	Sd.
8.2.16	Convoy. Company routine	Sd.
9.2.16	Convoy. Company routine	Sd.
10.2.16	Convoy. Company routine. Hot bath for all men of Coy.	Sd.
11.2.16	Convoy. Company routine. Pay Parade.	Sd.
12.2.16	Convoy. Company routine	Sd.
13.2.16	Church Parade.	Sd.
14.2.16	2/Lieut Charrington is attached to the Company and reports for duty. Lieut Morton, A.V.C. inspects all horses in Coy.	
	Convoy. Company routine	Sd.
15.2.16	Convoy. Company routine	Sd.
16.2.16	Convoy. Company routine	Sd.

Army Form C. 2118.

WAR DIARY
or
INTELLIGENCE SUMMARY.
(Erase heading not required.)

Instructions regarding War Diaries and Intelligence Summaries are contained in F. S. Regs., Part II. and the Staff Manual respectively. Title pages will be prepared in manuscript.

Hour, Date, Place	Summary of Events and Information	Remarks and references to Appendices
Warminster 17.2.16.	Convoy. Company routine. Hot bath for all men in Company.	&c.
" 18.2.16.	Convoy. Company routine. Car parade.	&c.
" 19.2.16.	Convoy. Company routine.	&c.
" 20.2.16.	Church Parade.	&c.
" 21.2.16.	Convoy. Company routine. Horses inspected by Lieut Moton. AVC	
" 22.2.16.	Company routine	
" 2.30 pm " "	Inspection of all horses of the Company by the Inspector of Remounts &c.	
" 23.2.16.	Horses destroyed which had been suffering from Pampura for the last three weeks.	
" 2.0. pm " "	Inspection of Transport by Major General London (C.I.G.M.G.S) &c. see App: 'A'.	
" 7. C. pm " "	Inspection of Company Books &c. by Major General London.	
" 10.30 am " "	Inspection of Cook House by Captain Blackwell.	&c.
" 11.30 am 24.2.16.	Inspection of Messing Book by Captain Blackwell.	
" 25.2.16	Convoy. Company routine. Hot baths for all men of Coy.	&c.
" 26.2.16	Convoy. Company routine.	&c.
" 27.2.16	Convoy. Company routine.	&c.
" 28.2.16.	Church parade.	&c.
" 29.2.16.	Convoy. Company routine.	&c.

S Norman Lt/Capt,
180th Infantry Brigade Co.

APPENDIX. 'A'

Inspection of Transport of this Company
by Major General. F.W.B. Landon. C.B.
(C.I.G.M.G.S.)

Major. General Landon inspected the
transport of this Company on February. 23.
1916. at 2-30 p.m.
2 Officers. 29 other ranks. 36. H.D. horses
10 riders and 18 wagons were on parade.
The wagons were paraded along the
BOREHAM. ROAD. WARMINSTER.
At 4:45 p.m. Major General Landon
inspected the Stables, harness room and
huts of the Company. and at 7 p.m
he inspected the books and general system
of the Company Office.

E. Wornum.
Lieut-

Confidential.

War Diary.

No. 4. Coy. 60th (London) Divisional Train.

From 1st March, 1916 to 31st March, 1916.

Army Form C. 2118.

WAR DIARY
INTELLIGENCE SUMMARY.
(Erase heading not required.)

March 1916.

Instructions regarding War Diaries and Intelligence Summaries are contained in F.S. Regs., Part II and the Staff Manual respectively. Title pages will be prepared in manuscript.

Hour, Date, Place	Summary of Events and Information	Remarks and references to Appendices
1.3.16 WARMINSTER	Convoy Brigade supplies as per Coy: orders. Colonel MORANT examined some of the books of the company.	R.S.
2.3.16 "	Convoy Brigade supplies as per Coy: orders examination of books continued by Colonel MORANT	R.S.
3.3.16 "	Convoy Brigade supplies as per Coy: orders examination of books etc continued by Colonel NASH.	R.S.
4.3.16 "	Capt C.Calver Smallwood returning from cruise at ALDERSHOT assumes command of the Company Captain SMALLWOOD appointed Member of Regimental Institute Committee. Convoy Brigade supplies as per Co. orders. Double issue.	R.S.
5.3.16 "	Church Parade. Inspection by O.C. stall Names Horses Wagons etc.	C.C.S.
6.3.16 "	Capt. SMALLWOOD Captain of the week. Convoy Brigade Supplies as per Co. orders. Col. NASH completes inspection of Cash Books & Mr Books &	C.C.S.

Army Form C. 2118.

WAR DIARY
or
INTELLIGENCE SUMMARY.
(Erase heading not required.)

Instructions regarding War Diaries and Intelligence Summaries are contained in F.S. Regs., Part II. and the Staff Manual respectively. Title pages will be prepared in manuscript.

Hour, Date, Place		Summary of Events and Information	Remarks and references to Appendices
March 7th	WARMINSTER.	Convoy Brigade Supplies, as per C.B. orders.	CCL.
8th	„	Convoy Brigade Supplies, as per C.o. orders.	CCL.
9th	„	Convoy Brigade Supplies as per C.o. orders. Inspection by G.O.C. 1st Lt. DUMAS. left on Sick leave. Officers Mess Meeting.	CCL.
10th	„	Convoy Brigade Supplies as per C.o. orders.	CCL.
11th	„	Convoy Brigade Supplies as per C.o. orders. Stable duties	CCL.
12th	„	Colonel Paul. Inspection by O.C. of all horses wagons harness &c.	CCL.
13th	„	Convoy Brigade Supplies as per C.o. orders. Capt. SMALLWOOD attended Lecture Demonstration. Capt. SMALLWOOD. to attend Musketry Course. Also 1 W.O. + 7 N.C.Os for 1 week. 2nd Lt. Redwood reported sick.	CCL.
14th	„	Convoy Brigade Supplies as per C.o. orders. 2nd Lt. Redwood proceeded on Sick leave.	CCL.
15th	„	Convoy Brigade Supplies as C.o. orders.	CCL.
16th	„	Convoy Brigade Supplies as per C.o. orders. Inspection of Train by D.A.Q.M.G.	CCL.
17th	„	Convoy Brigade Supplies as per C.o. orders.	CCL.

Army Form C. 2118.

WAR DIARY
or
INTELLIGENCE SUMMARY.
(Erase heading not required.)

March 1916 (cont?)

Hour, Date, Place	Summary of Events and Information	Remarks and references to Appendices
18th March 1916. WARMINSTER	Convoy for Brigade supplies as per Co. Orders. Double Leave.	CCS.
19th " "	Church Parade. Inspection of Horses by V.O. Inspection by O.C. of Horses vehicles harness &c	CCS.
20th " "	Convoy for Brigade supplies as per Co. orders. Lecture to O.C's by Major Meach on Discipline &c	CCS.
21st " "	Convoy for Brigade supplies as per Co. orders. 2 - 22 Rifles received from O.O. T.S. works for instructional purposes with Musketry Officers.	CCS.
22nd " "	Convoy for Brigade supplies as per Co. orders.	CCS.
23rd " "	Convoy for Brigade supplies as per Co. orders.	CCS.
24th " "	Convoy for Brigade supplies as per Co. orders. 2 Drivers sent Farriery Course at Romsey &c.	CCS.
25th " "	Convoy for Brigade supplies as per Co. orders. Stocktaking Board. 2/Lt. Redwood returned from Sick Leave. Double Leave.	CCS.
26th " "	Church Parade. O.C's Inspection of Horses harness &c	CCS.
27th " "	Convoy for Brigade supplies as per Co. orders. Capt. SMALLWOOD. Capt. & 2/Lt. DUMAS returned from sick leave.	CCS.
28th " "	Convoy Brigade supplies as per Co. orders.	CCS.
29th " "	Convoy Brigade supplies as per Co. orders	CCS.
30th " "	Drew 75 Rifles from 7/15 Batt. London Regiment. Convoy Brigade supplies as per Co. orders	CCS.
31st " "	Convoy for Brigade supplies as per Co. orders.	CCS. C Curshelwood Capt. O.C 181st Brigade Coy. A.S.C.

WAR DIARY
of the
579 Coy A.S.C.
From 1st March 1916 to 31st March 1916

Volume III   N°. 3.

WAR DIARY
or
INTELLIGENCE SUMMARY.
(Erase heading not required.)

Army Form C. 2118.

Instructions regarding War Diaries and Intelligence Summaries are contained in F. S. Regs., Part II and the Staff Manual respectively. Title pages will be prepared in manuscript.

Hour, Date, Place		Summary of Events and Information	Remarks and references to Appendices
Warminster	1.3.16	Convoy. Company routine. Colonel MORANT inspected books of the Company.	
"	2.3.16	Convoy. Company routine. Colonel MORANT inspected books of the Company. Hot baths for all men in Company.	do.
"	3.3.16	Convoy. Company routine.	do.
"	4.3.16	Convoy. Double issue. Company routine	do.
"	5.3.16	Church Parade. Inspection G.O.C. for all horses, harness, stables &c.	do.
"	6.3.16	Convoy. Company routine. &c.	do.
"	7.3.16	Convoy. Company routine. Major NASH inspected books of the Company	do.
"	8.3.16	Convoy. Company routine	do.
"	9.3.16	Convoy. Company routine. Inspection by G.O.C of all horses, stables, huts &c. Hot baths for men of Company.	do.

WAR DIARY
or
INTELLIGENCE SUMMARY.
(Erase heading not required.)

Army Form C. 2118.

Hour, Date, Place	Summary of Events and Information	Remarks and references to Appendices
Warminster. 10.3.16.	Coy. Company routine. Pay parade.	sd.
" 11.3.16.	Coy. Solo time. 40 rifles received. Company	sd.
" 12.3.16.	routine	sd.
" 13.3.16.	Church Parade.	
"	Coy. Company routine. Course of musketry for Officers and N.C.O's of Company started. Captain TAY returned from sick leave and resumed command.	sd.
" 14.3.16.	Coy. Company routine. Attended Lecture. N. Gassing.	w.f.j.
" 15.3.16	Coy. Company Routine. 2nd Lieut. Crossington left to report at Weymouth School of Cookery.	w.f.j.
" 16.3.16	Coy. Company Routine. Inspection of books etc by Major Carrath D.A.A.M.S.	w.f.j.

WAR DIARY
or
INTELLIGENCE SUMMARY.
(Erase heading not required.)

Army Form C. 2118.

Instructions regarding War Diaries and Intelligence Summaries are contained in F. S. Regs., Part II and the Staff Manual respectively. Title pages will be prepared in manuscript.

Hour, Date, Place	Summary of Events and Information	Remarks and references to Appendices
Westminster 17.3.16	Convoy Company Routine	W.S.J.
" 18.3.16	2nd Lieut. Champion returned from Weymouth. Convoy Company Routine.	W.S.J.
" 19.3.16	Convoy Company Routine. Church Parade. Inspection by S.O.	W.S.J.
" 20.3.16	2 horses names Carlo & 1st Lieut. HENLEY admitted to Hospital. Convoy Company Routine. Lecture by Major NASH.	W.S.J.
" 21.3.16	Convoy Company Routine	W.S.J.
" 22.3.16	Convoy Company Routine	W.S.J.
" 23.3.16	Convoy Company Routine	W.S.J.
" 24.3.16	Convoy Company Routine	W.S.J.
" 25.3.16	Convoy Company Routine. Preparing to take stock of all Unit's possessions	W.S.J.
" 26.3.16	Church Parade. Took stock of Wires in hands & Stores Issued.	W.S.J.

WAR DIARY
or
INTELLIGENCE SUMMARY.

(Erase heading not required.)

Army Form C. 2118.

Instructions regarding War Diaries and Intelligence Summaries are contained in F.S. Regs., Part II. and the Staff Manual respectively. Title pages will be prepared in manuscript.

Hour, Date, Place	Summary of Events and Information	Remarks and references to Appendices
Warminster 27.3.16	Convoy Company Routine for Sunday.	App. J.
" 28.3.16	Convoy Company Routine. 2 "Lieut Gamage attached for Instructions.	App. J.
" 29.3.16	Convoy Company Routine. 75 Rifles received from 2/8th London Regiment.	App. J.
" 30.3.16	Convoy Company Routine.	App. J.
" 31.3.16	Convoy Company Routine. attended F.A. Inspection 12 o'clock.	App. J.

W.S.A. Say. Capt.
519. Coy. A.S.C.
31st March 1916.

Confidential

War Diary.
of
520th (H.T.) Co A.S.C. — 60th (London) Divisional Train
from 1st April, 1916 to 30th April 1916.

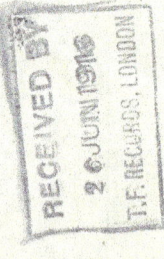

Army Form C. 2118.

WAR DIARY
or
INTELLIGENCE SUMMARY

April 1916.

(Erase heading not required.)

Instructions regarding War Diaries and Intelligence Summaries are contained in F.S. Regs., Part II and the Staff Manual respectively. Title pages will be prepared in manuscript.

Hour, Date, Place	Summary of Events and Information	Remarks and references to Appendices
1st April 1916. WARMINSTER.	Convoy for Brigade Supplies as per B. Orders - Double hune.	C.O.S.
2nd April 1916. Do.	Convoy for Brigade Supplies as per Co. Orders - O.C.s Inspection of Horses, harness &c.	C.O.S.
3rd April 1916. Do.	Convoy for Brigade Supplies as per Co. Orders - Alteration of title of Company to 520th. (H.T.) Coy. A.S.C. 60th (London) Divisional Train.	C.O.S.
4th April 1916. Do.	Convoy for Brigade Supplies as per Co. Orders. V.O. inspected all horses.	C.O.S.
5th April 1916. Do.	Convoy for Brigade Supplies as per Co. Orders.	C.O.S.
6th April 1916. Do.	Convoy for Brigade Supplies as per Co. Orders. Rec'd 20 Rds. 303 Ball (each.)	C.O.S.
7th April 1916. Do.	Convoy for Brigade Supplies as per Co. Orders. Rec'd 1 Rifle ex 2/19th.	C.O.S.
8th April 1916. Do.	Convoy for Brigade Supplies as per Co. Orders. Double hune.	C.O.S.
9th April 1916. Do.	Church Parade. O.C's Inspection of all Horses, Harness, &c.	C.O.S.
10th April 1916. Do.	Convoy for Brigade Supplies as per Co. Orders. M.O. inspected the teeth of the men of the Coy. Preliminary Musketry Instruction.	C.O.S.

WAR DIARY
or
INTELLIGENCE SUMMARY.

(Erase heading not required.)

Army Form C. 2118.

April 1916 (Cont.)

Hour, Date, Place	Summary of Events and Information	Remarks and references to Appendices
11th April 1916. WARMINSTER	Convoy as per Co Orders for Brigade Supplies. Inspection of Unserviceable Equipment by D.A.D.O.S.	CCI.
12th " "	Convoy for Brigade Supplies as per Co Orders. Inspection of Horses for Casting by A.D.V.S. — 1 Cast Bach Troy Mare No. 73. Ordered Hospital at Mulford Mews Mare No. 59. Capt SMALLWOOD allowed R.T.O's office for Instruction in Intraining	CCI.
13th April 1916 "	Convoy for Brigade Supplies as per Co Orders. Issue of Overcoats Boots Huts specially Scrubbed out & disinfected by M.O's Orders.	CCI.
14th " "	Convoy for Brigade Supplies as per Co Orders. Cap.	CCI.
15th " "	Convoy for Brigade Supplies as per Co Orders. Double Issue. Captain SMALLWOOD Presented at Court of Enquiry into illegal absence of No. 2501. Driver Leitch W.J. — 2300 - 303. Roll Cartridges Rec? on M.O. Rec? EMERGENCY SYSTEM	CCI.
16th " "	Church Parade. O.C? Inspection of Horses Huts Harness & Huts again specially washed & disinfected. Kit Inspection	CCI.
17th " "	Convoy for Brigade Supplies as per Co Orders. Capt. SMALLWOOD in charge of Foot Drill for w/e 23rd April. Received 1650 rounds. 22 Cartridges (1500 short as per Voucher & P.N. etc.) Clothing Ledger to Local Auditor.	CCI.

WAR DIARY
or
INTELLIGENCE SUMMARY.

April 1916. (cont.)

Army Form C. 2118.

(Erase heading not required.)

Hour, Date, Place	Summary of Events and Information	Remarks and references to Appendices
18th March 1916. WARMINSTER	Convoy for Brigade Supplies - as per Co. Orders.	ccl.
19th "	Convoy for Brigade Supplies - as per Co. Orders - Double teams	ccs.
20th "	Convoy for Brigade Supplies as per Co. Orders - Double teams	ccl.
21st "	Good Friday - Church Parade.	ccl.
22nd "	Convoy for Brigade Supplies as per Co. orders. - Double teams	ccs.
23rd "	Easter Sunday - Church Parade - Inspection by O.C. of Horses an	ccl.
24th "	Easter Bank Holiday. - Capt. SMALLWOOD - Capt. of the Week.	ccl.
25th "	Convoy for Brigade Supplies - Draft of 110 Men from 3rd Line transferred. 5 Heavy Draught Horses received from Remount Depôt Leighton Buzzard	ccl.
26th "	Convoy for Brigade Supplies - as per Co. Orders. Drew 7. Bicycles & Resistro Ammunition for Practice. Horse Aux No. 176 Renvoi out killed	ccl.
27th "	Convoy for Brigade Supplies - as per co orders.	ccl.
28th "	Convoy for Brigade Supplies - as per Co. orders, as Capt. of the week. Capt. SMALLWOOD on duty during weighing of Horses, Wagons & Personnel of 518th Co. during the weight & also Brigade Transport	ccl.
29th "	Convoy for Brigade Supplies - as per Company Orders.	ccl.
30th "	Convoy for Brigade Supplies - as per Company Orders	ccl.

C. Colvin Smallwood

WAR DIARY.

of the

519th Coy. A.S.C.

From April 1st 1916 to April 30th 1916.

Volume III.   No 4.

Page 1.

Army Form C. 2118.

WAR DIARY
or
INTELLIGENCE SUMMARY.
(Erase heading not required.)

Instructions regarding War Diaries and Intelligence Summaries are contained in F.S. Regs., Part II and the Staff Manual respectively. Title pages will be prepared in manuscript.

Hour, Date, Place	Summary of Events and Information	Remarks and references to Appendices
Shorncliffe 1.4.16.	Coy. Company Routine.	F.O.C.
" 2.4.16.	Church Parade. Inspection F.O.C of all Horses, harness, saddles etc.	W.F.O.
" 3.4.16.	Coy. Company Routine.	W.F.O.
" 4.4.16.	Coy. C. Hogans F. Quarters Coy to Boyton	W.F.O.
" 5.4.16.	Coy. C. Hogans F. Quarters Coy to Boyton Company Routine.	W.F.O.
" 6.4.16.	Coy 2. Hogans No. 2 Coy Company Routine.	W.F.O.
" 7.4.16.	All Men on Musketry. Pay Parade. Lieut. Wornum on sick leave.	W.F.O.
" 8.4.16.	All Men on Musketry. S. Rounds fired Miniature Range.	W.F.O.
" 9.4.16.	Church Parade. Inspection by F.O.C.	W.F.O.

Page 2
Army Form C. 2118.

WAR DIARY
or
INTELLIGENCE SUMMARY.
(Erase heading not required.)

Hour, Date, Place	Summary of Events and Information	Remarks and references to Appendices
Hannington 10.4.16.	Convoy. 3 Wagons 9½ H. Coy. Inspection by C.O. Carbines Clothes for Shalts. Company Routine.	w.s.f.
" 11.4.16.	Convoy. 3 Wagons 9½ Coy. Company Routine.	w.s.f.
" 12.4.16.	Convoy. Musketry all men not having previously attended Company Routine.	w.s.f.
" 13.4.16.	Convoy. Aiden School. Company Routine.	w.s.f.
" 14.4.16.	Convoy. 1 Wagon received from 2/9th Regiment. Company Routine. Pay Parade.	w.s.f.
" 15.4.16.	Convoy. Company Routine. Church Parade. Lieut. WORNUM returned from Sick leave. 2nd Lieut. CHARRINGTON	w.s.f.
" 16.4.16	returned from Transport course ALDERSHOT.	w.s.f.

Page 3

Army Form C. 2118.

WAR DIARY
or
INTELLIGENCE SUMMARY.
(Erase heading not required.)

Instructions regarding War Diaries and Intelligence Summaries are contained in F. S. Regs., Part II. and the Staff Manual respectively. Title pages will be prepared in manuscript.

Hour, Date, Place	Summary of Events and Information	Remarks and references to Appendices
WARMINSTER 17.4.16.	Company routine. Convoy.	do.
" 18.4.16.	Captain JAY reported at ALDERSHOT for course of Instruction and Lieut WORNUM take command during his absence.	
" 19.4.16.	Company routine. Convoy.	
" 20.4.16.	Double issue. Convoy. Company routine.	do.
" 21.4.16.	Double issue. Convoy. Company routine. Baths for all men in Coy.	do.
" 22.4.16.	Church Parade. Company routine.	do.
" 23.4.16.	Double issue. Convoy. Company routine.	do.
" 24.4.16.	Church Parade. Company routine. 6 H.D. horses (known as Heavy Draught) horses received from MAIDENHEAD. S.H.D. horses from FORT BROCKHURST. and S.H.D. horse from CHANDLERSFORD. Here had been taken in the strength of the Coy. Coy routine.	do.
" 25.4.16.	Convoy. Six men reported from 3rd line and taken on strength of A Company. Company routine.	do.
" 26.4.16.	Convoy. Company routine. Football for whole Coy.	do.
" 27.4.16.	Convoy. Company routine. C.S.M. EMERSON kicked by horse and has two crushed Hot Baths for Coy.	do.
" 28.4.16.	Convoy. Coy routine. Five pigeons despatched for (30th INF. BDE HDQRS. SW.)	do.

Page 4.

Army Form C. 2118.

WAR DIARY
or
INTELLIGENCE SUMMARY.
(Erase heading not required.)

Instructions regarding War Diaries and Intelligence Summaries are contained in F.S. Regs., Part II. and the Staff Manual respectively. Title pages will be prepared in manuscript.

Hour, Date, Place	Summary of Events and Information	Remarks and references to Appendices
WARMINSTER 29.4.16.	Convoy. Received orders to prepare to move. 3 Baggage wagons with 1 day iron ration attached to each Battalion. 1 wagon to Brigade HdQrs. Ammunition and full establishment as previously issued.	
" 30.4.16.	Church Parade. Company ready to move. Convoy.	

S. Warren. Capt.
79th M.T. Coy. ASC

Confidential.

War Diary.

of

520th (H.T.) Co. A.S.C. - 60th (London) Divisional Train.

from 1st May, 1916 to 31st May, 1916.

WAR DIARY
or
INTELLIGENCE SUMMARY.
(Erase heading not required.)

Army Form C. 2118.

May, 1916.

Hour, Date, Place	Summary of Events and Information	Remarks and references to Appendices
1st May, 1916. WARMINSTER	Convoy for Brigade Supplies as per Company orders. Lecture by O.C. to men of Coy on Methods of Transport over Seas &c.	CCL.
2nd Do	Convoy for Brigade Supplies & as per Company orders. Continuation of Lecture by O.C. & General Instruction to them as to Overseas work & on move.	CCL.
3rd Do	Convoy for Brigade Supplies as per Company Orders. Instruction by O.C. in use of Anti-Gas Helmets.	CCL.
4th Do	Convoy for Brigade Supplies as per Co. orders. Capt. SMALLWOOD President of Board of Officers to enquire into damage done by a pair of runaways belonging to 517th Co. Inspection by Capt. SMALLWOOD of 9/6th Field Ambulance Equipment, Horses & preparatory to taking over same.	CCL.
5th Do	Convoy for Brigade Supplies as as Co. orders. All Leave Suspended	CCL.
6th Do	Convoy for Brigade Supplies as per Co. orders. Double Issue.	CCL.
7th Do	Church Parade. Inspection by O.C. of all Wagons, Horses, Harness &c.	CCL.
8th Do	Convoy for Brigade Supplies as per Co. orders. The Coy Started Firing Course at Longbridge Deverill Range.	CCL.
9th Do	Convoy for Brigade Supplies as per Coy. Orders. Continuation of Firing Course	CCL.

Army Form C. 2118.

WAR DIARY
or
INTELLIGENCE SUMMARY.   May. 1916 (cont?)

(Erase heading not required.)

Instructions regarding War Diaries and Intelligence Summaries are contained in F.S. Regs., Part II. and the Staff Manual respectively. Title pages will be prepared in manuscript.

Hour, Date, Place	Summary of Events and Information	Remarks and references to Appendices
10th May.16. WARMINSTER	Convoy for Brigade Supplies as per Co. Orders. Mr Lt. REDWOOD proceeded to ALDERSHOT for Instructional Course. Firing continued.	CCI.
11th D°.	Convoy for Brigade Supplies as per Co. Orders. Firing Course continued.	CCI.
12th D°.	Convoy for Brigade Supplies as per Co. Orders. Firing Course Completed.	CCI.
13th D°.	Convoy for Brigade Supplies as per Co. Orders. Double Issue.	CCI.
14th D°.	Convoy for Brigade Supplies as per Co. Orders.	CCI.
15th D°.	Church Parade. Inspection of Horses, Harness Stables by O.C.	CCI.
15th D°.	Convoy for Brigade Supplies as per Co. Orders. 2 Goggles. Anti-Gas received for Instructional Purposes. Sergt WITHERS proceeded home for Instruction.	CCI.
16th D°.	Convoy for Brigade Supplies as per Co. Orders.	CCI.
17th D°.	Convoy for Brigade Supplies as per Co. Orders. 20 R.D. rec'd from 517th Co.	CCI.
18th D°.	Convoy for Brigade Supplies as per Co. Orders.	CCI.
19th D°.	Convoy for Brigade Supplies as per Co. Orders.	CCI.
20th D°.	Convoy for Brigade Supplies as per Co. Orders. Double Issue.	CCI.
21st D°.	Church Parade. Inspection by O.I. of all harness horses Stables.	CCI.
22nd D°.	Convoy for Brigade Supplies as per Co. Orders. Capt. SMALLWOOD Capt. of the week for following week.	CCI.

WAR DIARY
or
INTELLIGENCE SUMMARY.

Army Form C. 2118.

May 1916 (Cont.)

(Erase heading not required.)

Hour, Date, Place		Summary of Events and Information	Remarks and references to Appendices
23rd May 1916	WARMINSTER	Convoy for Brigade Supplies & as per Co. Orders. Double issue.	CRS.
24th	Do	Divisional Route March & Inspection by G.O.C. at same. Sec. Lt. BRANDER. posted as Requisitioning officer.	CRS.
25th	Do	Convoy for Brigade Supplies. 2nd Lt. REDWOOD returned to Duty from Course at ALDERSHOT.	CRS.
26th	Do	Convoy for Brigade Supplies as per Co. Orders.	CRS.
27th	Do	Convoy for Brigade Supplies & as per Co. Orders. Double issue.	CRS.
28th	Do	Church Parade. Parch Pockets for Anti-gas Helmets rec'd. & issued with instructions. Inspection by O.C. of all horses, Wagons, Harness. Capt. SMALLWOOD completed weeks Tour of Duty as Captain Mid Week.	CRS.
29th	Do	Convoy for Brigade Supplies & as per Co. Orders. Mare No 1024 (in foal) sent to Mr. Wallis' Farm at Corton on agreement. Prtns. D.A.D.R.	CRS.
30th	Do	Convoy for Brigade Supplies & as per Co. Orders. 120 Rds. S.A. Wolsley rec'd. for Practice Purposes. Inspection by G.O.C. at North Farm.	CRS.
31st	Do	Convoy for Brigade Supplies as per Co. Orders. Inspection by His Majesty. The King at North Farm.	CRS.

C. Calvin Smallwood
Capt.
Add. 520th (H.T.) Coy. A.S.

Volume 3

WAR DIARY
INTELLIGENCE SUMMARY
(Erase heading not required.)

Army Form C. 2118.

Hour, Date, Place		Summary of Events and Information	Remarks and references to Appendices
Warminster	1.5.16.	Convoy. Company routine. Standing by awaiting orders from Bn.	Sd.
"	2.5.16	Convoy. Company routine. Standing by awaiting orders from Bn.	Sd.
"	3.5.16.	Convoy. Wagon attached to Battalion recalled and own ration returned.	Sd.
"	4.5.16.	Convoy. Company routine. Received 1 MK × G.S. wagon complete Stables & took over transport details of 4th Batt. for men electric horses.	Sd.
"	5.5.16	2/5 Field Ambulance. Company routine. Entire stable in charge transport details of 2/5 Field Ambulance.	Sd.
"	6.5.16.	Convoy. Company routine.	Sd.
"	7.5.16.	Church Parade. Company routine. Captain J.A.Y. return from course of instruction at Salisbury. ALDERSHOT and assumes command of company.	Sd.
"	8.5.16.	Convoy. Musketry. Rifle Range Team.	W.S.J.
"	9.5.16.	Convoy. Musketry. Rifle Range Team.	W.S.J.
"	10.5.16.	Convoy. Company Routine.	W.S.J.
"	11.5.16.	Convoy. Musketry. Company Routine.	W.S.J.
"	12.5.16.	Convoy. Pay Parade.	W.S.J.

WAR DIARY or INTELLIGENCE SUMMARY

Army Form C. 2118.

(Erase heading not required.)

Instructions regarding War Diaries and Intelligence Summaries are contained in F.S. Regs., Part II. and the Staff Manual respectively. Title Pages will be prepared in manuscript.

Place	Date	Hour	Summary of Events and Information	Remarks and references to Appendices
Warminster	13/5/16		Convoy Double road. Church went. 179th Brigade. Camp return of 179th Brigade from Ireland.	nop. 8
"	14/5/16		Church Parade. Inspection by C.O. return of 179th Brigade	no. 8
"	15/5/16		Convoy Company Routine. Four from vehicle sheds on Rinos	no. 8
"	16/5/16		Convoy Company Routine	no. 8
"	17/5/16		Convoy Company Routine	no. 8
"	18/5/16		Convoy Company Routine	no. 8
"	19/5/16		Convoy Pay Parade. return from Hospital of Cpl EPPY	no. 8
"	20/5/16		Convoy Double road.	no. 8
"	21/6/16		Church Parade	no. 8
"	22/5/16		Convoy Company Routine	no. 1
"	23/6/16		Convoy Double road. Barrage Weapons Infantry Battalion	no. 8

Army Form C. 2118.

WAR DIARY
or
INTELLIGENCE SUMMARY

(Erase heading not required.)

Instructions regarding War Diaries and Intelligence Summaries are contained in F. S. Regs., Part II. and the Staff Manual respectively. Title Pages will be prepared in manuscript.

Place	Date	Hour	Summary of Events and Information	Remarks and references to Appendices
Dunmurry	24.5.16		Divisional Route March. no casualties.	m.s.s.
"	25.5.16		Convoy. Coal Carting. Company Routine.	m.s.s.
"	26.5.16		Convoy. Coal & Clinker Carting. Company Routine.	m.s.s.
"	27.5.16		Convoy. Route Drill. Company Routine.	m.s.s.
"	28.5.16		Church Parade. Inspection by C.O.	m.s.s.
"	29.5.16		Convoy. Coal Carting. Company Routine.	m.s.s.
"	30.5.16		Convoy. Preliminary Inspection at NORTHS. FARM by G.O.C. ?	m.s.s.
"	31.5.16		Inspection of Division by HIS MAJESTY. Convoy at 3 P.M.	m.s.s.

W.F.A. Ray. Capt.
519th S.T. Coy. A.S.C.
31st May. 1916.

War Diary
of the
519th M.T. Coy. A.S.C.
from June 1st 1916 to June 21st 1916.

Volume III. N° 6.

Army Form C. 2118.

WAR DIARY
or
INTELLIGENCE SUMMARY
(Erase heading not required.)

Instructions regarding War Diaries and Intelligence Summaries are contained in F. S. Regs., Part II. and the Staff Manual respectively. Title Pages will be prepared in manuscript.

Place	Date	Hour	Summary of Events and Information	Remarks and references to Appendices
Farmoutiers	1.6.16.		Convoy. Company Routine. Ten days Special Leave commenced.	nort. J.
"	2.6.16.		Convoy. Company Routine.	nort. J.
"	3.6.16.		Convoy. Company Routine.	nort. J.
"	4.6.16.		Convoy. Company Routine.	nort. J.
"	5.6.16.		Convoy. Inspection of First Line Transport by GENERAL LANDON.	nort. J.
"	6.6.16.		Inspection of Company by GENERAL LANDON. Convoy 16 Boyton.	nort. J.
"	7.6.16.		Convoy. Company Routine.	nort. J.
"	8.6.16.		Convoy. Company Routine. LIEUTENANT WORNUM on Ten days leave.	nort. J.
"	9.6.16.		Convoy. 10 Wagons Boyton. Company Routine.	nort. J.
"	10.6.16.		Convoy. Company Routine.	nort. J.

2449 Wt. W14957/M90 750,000 1/16 J.B.C. & A. Forms/C.2118/12.

Army Form C. 2118.

WAR DIARY
or
INTELLIGENCE SUMMARY
(Erase heading not required.)

Instructions regarding War Diaries and Intelligence Summaries are contained in F. S. Regs., Part II. and the Staff Manual respectively. Title Pages will be prepared in manuscript.

Place	Date	Hour	Summary of Events and Information	Remarks and references to Appendices
Warminster	1/6/16		Convoy. Company Routine. Bers of Overseas Kit.	Wt. J.
"	12/6/16		Convoy. Company Routine.	Wt. J.
"	13/6/16		Convoy. Company Routine. Officers Mess Meeting.	Wt. J.
"	14/6/16		Convoy. Company Routine. Boards on Clothing.	Wt. J.
"	15/6/16		Convoy. Company Routine.	Wt. J.
"	16/6/16		Convoy. Company Routine.	Wt. J.
"	17/6/16		Convoy. Company Routine.	Wt. J.
"	18/6/16		Convoy. Company Routine.	Wt. J.
"	19/6/16		Convoy. Inspection of Company by C.O. Inspection of all men of Company by M.O.	Wt. J.
"	20/6/16		Convoy. (Detailed issue)	Wt. J.

Army Form C. 2118.

WAR DIARY
INTELLIGENCE SUMMARY
(Erase heading not required.)

Instructions regarding War Diaries and Intelligence Summaries are contained in F.S. Regs., Part II. and the Staff Manual respectively. Title Pages will be prepared in manuscript.

Place	Date	Hour	Summary of Events and Information	Remarks and references to Appendices
Warminster	2/6/16.		Convoy. Preparing for Embarkation.	Examinister J.

2449 Wt. W14957/M90 750,000 1/16 J.B.C. & A. Forms/C.2118/12.

Confidential

War Diary

of

520th (H.T.) Co. A.S.C. - 60th (London) Divisional Train
1st at Col.
1st June, 1916. to 30th June, 1916.

Army Form C. 2118.

WAR DIARY
or
INTELLIGENCE SUMMARY.
(Erase heading not required.)

June 1916.

Instructions regarding War Diaries and Intelligence Summaries are contained in F.S. Regs., Part II and the Staff Manual respectively. Title pages will be prepared in manuscript.

Hour, Date, Place	Summary of Events and Information	Remarks and references to Appendices
WARMINSTER 1st June 1916.	Convoy for Brigade supplies & as per Co. orders. Trial 4 days leave granted, to finishes by 12th June 1916.	Col.
Do. 2nd Do.	Convoy for Brigade supplies & as per Co. orders.	Col.
Do. 3rd Do.	Convoy for Brigade supplies & as per Co. orders. Horses nos. 47 + 75.	Col.
Do. 4th Do.	Convoy for Brigade supplies & as per Co. orders.	Col.
Do. 5th Do.	Capt. SMALLWOOD proceeds on 10 days leave. Company Temporarily hands over to 2nd Lt. DUMAS. Convoy for Brigade supplies as per Co. orders. 2nd Lt. Dumas was Present at inspection of Station transport by Maj. G.H.C. Lanau. Inspection of Station Trans. Capt. SMALLWOOD returned.	Col. R.S. Col.
Do. 6th Do.	Convoy for Brigade supplies & as per Co. orders. Inspection by Major Linwood Louson C.I.Q.M.G.S.	Col.
Do. 7th Do.	Convoy for Brigade supplies & as per Co. orders.	Col.
Do. 8th Do.	Convoy for Brigade supplies & as per Co. orders.	Col.
Do. 9th Do.	Convoy for Brigade supplies & as per Co. orders. Capt. SMALLWOOD proceeds on 10 days leave - Company hands over to Capt W.H. WHITTINGTON	Col.

WAR DIARY or INTELLIGENCE SUMMARY

Army Form C. 2118.

June 1916.

Place	Hour, Date	Summary of Events and Information	Remarks and references to Appendices
WARMINSTER	10th June 1916	Convoy for Brigade Supplies as per C. ORders. Capt. WHITTINGTON and 2/Lt REDWOOD was present at the inspection of the horses of the Co. by Brigadier-General Bridge.	
Do	11th do	Convoy for Brigade Supplies as per C. Orders. Convoy of 10 Wagons to Boyton Camp for Lincolnshires Troops.	
Do	12th do	Convoy for Brigade Supplies as per C. Orders. Expiration of June holiday leave. On arrival at 12 o'clock all men duly reported.	
Do	13th do	Convoy for Brigade Supplies as per C. Orders. Attendance reported. Capt. SMALLWOOD returned from leave & took over command of C.B. from Capt. WHITTINGTON. Preparation for Board of Enquiry on Clothing &c.	
Do	14th do	Convoy for Brigade supplies as per Company Orders Capt. SMALLWOOD President of Board of Officers on Surplus Clothing &c. Overseer Kit Inspection. Certificate as to Stores & sundries to the Orderly Room as to Clothing, Equipment, Ordnance Stores &c.	
Do	15th do	Convoy for Brigade Supplies &c as per Company Orders. Returned all fair worn, condemned & new clothing. Returned Water Cart Mark V to O.O. Warminster. Capt. SMALLWOOD attended a Conference at R.T.O. Office re Entrainment of Units.	

WAR DIARY
or
INTELLIGENCE SUMMARY.

(Erase heading not required.)

Army Form C. 2118.

Instructions regarding War Diaries and Intelligence Summaries are contained in F.S. Regs., Part II. and the Staff Manual respectively. Title pages will be prepared in manuscript.

Hour, Date, Place	Summary of Events and Information	Remarks and references to Appendices
16th June 1916. WARMINSTER.	Convoys for Brigade Supplies & as per Company Orders. Embarkation States received. Received Orders that Pack Detachment would entrain with Co. Received notes for guidance for Embarkation.	C.O.
17th June 1916. Do.	Convoys for Brigade Supplies & as per Company Orders. Obtained all Surplus Ammunition to O.C. Warminster. Received Embarkation Orders. Received Notes for Instruction for Entrainment Pts I & II.	C.O.
18th June 1916. Do.	Convoys for Brigade Supplies & as per Company Orders. Pack Detachment embarkation with the Co. cancelled. Orders received to return Wagon & for the M.G. Coy. rec'd orders re Marching out State.	C.O.
19th June 1916. Do.	Convoys for Brigade Supplies & as per Company Orders. Capt. SMALLWOOD on duty as Capt. of the Week for the ensuing week. Supply Section Lorries reported for duty on Wagon Lines.	C.O.
20th June 1916. Do.	Convoys &c. Inspection of all Ranks by M.O. Inspection of all horses, harness, vehicles, equipment take place in full marching order being final inspection for Overseas as Company Mobilizing.	C.O.
21st June 1916. Do.	Convoys for Brigade Supplies & as per Company Orders. C.O. & Adjutant proceed overseas. Command of remainder of Train handed over to Capt. SMALLWOOD. 517th H.T. Co. also proceed overseas.	C.O.

Army Form C. 2118.

WAR DIARY
or
INTELLIGENCE SUMMARY.
(Erase heading not required.)

Instructions regarding War Diaries and Intelligence Summaries are contained in F.S. Regs., Part II. and the Staff Manual respectively. Title pages will be prepared in manuscript.

Hour, Date, Place	Summary of Events and Information	Remarks and references to Appendices
22nd June 1916 WARMINSTER.	Brigade Convoys to arrive Company orders 518th H.T.Co A.S.C. proceed overseas.	CO.-
23rd June 1916. Do.	Supply Wagon with overseas Rations proceed to (Units & remained with them. Brigade supplied to/for Company Convoy orders — 519th H.T.Co. proceed overseas	CO.-
24th to Do. 26th Do.	Superintended despatch of 1st line Transport of 181st Brigade. 520th H.T.Co. A.S.C. entrained for overseas all documents, horse lines & Clearers in Nolts Camp Warminster.	CO.-
	Cart handed over o/c Details.	

Calder Mullins
Capt.
O.C. 528th(H.T) Coy. A.S.C.

CONFIDENTIAL

WAR DIARY
- of -
60TH (LONDON) DIVISIONAL, A.S.C.

From:- 20TH June 1916 ~ To:- 30TH June 1916

VOLUME I   No: (1).

TRAIN
VOL I

Army Form C. 2118

WAR DIARY
or
INTELLIGENCE SUMMARY
(Erase heading not required.)

Instructions regarding War Diaries and Intelligence Summaries are contained in F.S. Regs., Part II. and the Staff Manual respectively. Title Pages will be prepared in manuscript.

Place	Date	Hour	Summary of Events and Information	Remarks and references to Appendices
WARMINSTER	20th 16th 24th		Instructions for Embarkation of Division received on the 16th June. The following is a résumé of the arrangements made for baggage wagons to join units and for the issue of overseas rations. All baggage wagons were despatched to units on the evening of the day previous to the day of Embarkation. Overseas rations were issued to units from the WARMINSTER Supply Depot according to time table attached under Appendix II. To units located more than 3 miles from the WARMINSTER Supply Depot the baggage wagons were utilised to convey the feed rations for the following day, Supply wagons being loaded with the overseas rations. Instructions to units and time tables were published & the O.C. Train on the 17th inst. Nothing occurred to interfere with the smooth working of the arrangements.	APPENDIX I Programme of Entrainment II (a) II (b)

WAR DIARY
or
INTELLIGENCE SUMMARY
(Erase heading not required.)

Army Form C. 2118

Instructions regarding War Diaries and Intelligence Summaries are contained in F.S. Regs., Part II. and the Staff Manual respectively. Title Pages will be prepared in manuscript.

Place	Date	Hour	Summary of Events and Information	Remarks and references to Appendices
TRAIN HDQRS.	23rd	3 p.m.	Train Headquarters opened at FLERS in the concentration area. Detaining Echelon of the Train at ST. POL and PETIT HOUDAIN. A portion of the supply Column arrived and was billeted at TINQUES. Arrangements made by S.S.O. for grouping of units and distribution of bag. O.C. Train reconnoitred and selected suitable refilling points.	
FLERS.	24th	10 a.m.	No 1 (Headquarters) Coy. detrained at ST. POL and proceeded to MONTS EN-TERNOIS. Units arriving in the same day are placed in Group A.	
		6 p.m.	O.C. No 1 Coy collected supply wagons of units in Group A during the night.	
FLERS.	25th	7 a.m.	Column (Section A) arrived and dumped at R.P. on the ST. POL - FREVENT road. 2 miles N.E. of NUNCQ.	
		8.30.	Group A refilled and was completed by 10 a.m.	
		3 p.m.	No 2 Coy. detrained at ST. POL and marched to DOFFINE. Supply details no 2 coy. to MCQ.	

WAR DIARY or INTELLIGENCE SUMMARY

Army Form C. 2118

Place	Date	Hour	Summary of Events and Information	Remarks and references to Appendices
HQ R.S. TRAIN.				
FLERS.	26th	7a.m.	Supply column (section A) dumped at R.P. on ST.POL – FREVENT road.	Appendix III
		7.30–	" (section B) dumped at R.P. at A.C.Q. for units of 179th Bde which have proceed their to 51 Div. area.	
		8.30a.m.	Refilling continued and was completed at 10.15 a.m.	
		12 Noon.	No 2 Coy. turns from DOFFINE to A.C.Q. for group B.	
		10 p.m.	No 3 Coy debuses at ST.POL and marched to HAUTE COTE. No 26th groups but No 3 Coy. in group C. All units arriving in group C.	
FLERS.	27th	7.30a.m.	Supply column dumped at following refilling points :— Group A at the TERNAS – MAZIERES road. Head of R.P. at x roads 500 S.W. of A in AVERDOIN ST. Group B at A.C.Q. Group C. on the FREVENT – ST. POL road.	Appendix IV
		8.30 a.m.	Refilling commenced and completed by 10.10 a.m.	
		11 a.m.	No 4 Coy detrains at ST.POL and marches to CHELERS. All units arriving on 27th groups met No 4 Coy. in groups. D	

WAR DIARY
or
INTELLIGENCE SUMMARY
(Erase heading not required.)

Army Form C. 2118

Place	Date	Hour	Summary of Events and Information	Remarks and references to Appendices
TRAIN HQRS.	23rd	3 p.m.	Train Headquarters opened at FLERS in the concentration area. Detraining echelon of the Division at ST. POL and PETIT HOUDAIN. A portion of the supply column arrived and was billeted at TINQUES. Arrangements made by S.S.O. for grouping of units and distribution of bag. O.C. Train reconnoitres and selects suitable repelling points.	
FLERS.	24th	10 a.m.	No.1 (Headquarter) Coy. detrained at ST. POL and proceeded to MONTS EN-TERNOIS.	
		6 p.m.	Units arriving on the same day are placed in Group A. O.C. No.1 Coy corrected supply wagons of units in Group A during the night.	
FLERS.	25th	7 a.m.	Column (Echelon A) arrived and dumped at R.P. on the ST. POL - FREVENT road, 2 miles N.E. of NUNCQ.	
		8.30.	Group A receives and was completed by 10 a.m.	
		3 p.m.	No. 2 Coy. detrained at ST. POL and marched to DOFFINE. Supply attack No 2 Coy to MCQ.	

… Army Form C. 2118

WAR DIARY
or
INTELLIGENCE SUMMARY
(Erase heading not required.)

Instructions regarding War Diaries and Intelligence Summaries are contained in F.S. Regs., Part II. and the Staff Manual respectively. Title Pages will be prepared in manuscript.

Place	Date	Hour	Summary of Events and Information	Remarks and references to Appendices
TRAIN. H.Q. & R.S.				
FLERS.	26th	7 a.m.	Supply column (section A) dumped at R.P. on ST POL – FREVENT road.	Appendix III
		7.30 —	" (section B) dumped at R.P. at A.C.B. to units C 179. By Mrs. which have proceeded there to 51 Div. area.	
		8.30 a.m. 12 noon 1.0 p.m.	Refilling commenced and was completed at 10.15 a.m. No 2 coy. turns from POFFINE to A.C.B. for groups B. No 3 coy debussed at ST POL and marched to HAUTE COTE. All units arriving on 26th groups out as 3 coy. in groups C.	
FLERS.	27th	7.30 a.m.	Supply column dumped at following refilling points :— Groups A & HQ TERNAS – MAIZIERES road. heads of R.P. at X roads 500 S.W. of A in AVERDOIN RT. Groups B at A.C.B. Groups C on the FREVENT – ST POL road.	Appendix IV
		8.30 a.m.	Refilling commenced and completed 10.10 a.m.	
		11 a.m.	No 4 coy detrained at ST POL and marched to CHELERS. All units arriving on 27th groups out as groups D No 4 coy. in groups D	

WAR DIARY
or
INTELLIGENCE SUMMARY
(Erase heading not required.)

Army Form C. 2118

Instructions regarding War Diaries and Intelligence Summaries are contained in F. S. Regs., Part II. and the Staff Manual respectively. Title Pages will be prepared in manuscript.

Place	Date	Hour	Summary of Events and Information	Remarks and references to Appendices
	28ᵗʰ	7.30 a.m.	Column arrived and dumped at extreme points as follows:— Groups A, C, and D on the TINQUES — SAVY road. Just E of extreme TINQUES. Group B at A.C.D.	Appendix V
		8.30 a.m.	Refilling commenced and was completed by 10.30 a.m.	
		2 p.m.	No 1 (Headquarters) Coy. moves from MONTS-EN-TERNOIS to TINQUES. No 2 — — HAUTE-COTE. No 3 Coy — — to DOFFINE.	
	29ᵗʰ	7.30 a.m.	Column arrived and dumped at extreme points as follows:— C and D at TINQUES. B at A.C.D. A(x) at HAUTE AVESNES.	Appendix VI
		12 noon	Headquarters of train moved from FLERS to TINQUES.	
		1 p.m.	Reinforcement of No 1 (illegible) Coy. moved from TINQUES to HAUTE-AVESNES for Divl. Troops in 51ˢᵗ Divl. area.	

Army Form C. 2118

WAR DIARY
or
INTELLIGENCE SUMMARY
(Erase heading not required.)

Instructions regarding War Diaries and Intelligence Summaries are contained in F.S. Regs., Part II. and the Staff Manual respectively. Title Pages will be prepared in manuscript.

Place	Date	Hour	Summary of Events and Information	Remarks and references to Appendices
	30th	7.30 a.m.	Column arrived and detrained. Proceeded from ao to 29 C. Group A. and Group B. and detrained into A. and M2. A. retained from at II HAUTE-AVESNES. Proceeded Div. Train Companies as to 29 C. No incidents to record.	Appendices VII Appendix VI

In the Field.
1/7/16

[signature]
Capt & DTO
60TH (LONDON) DIVISIONAL, A.S.C.

APPENDIX I   C/155/2

SECRET
PROGRAMME NO: 32
                        Order of Embarkation 60th Division

Index No.	UNIT	From	To
	June 18th		
I	Divisional Supply Column	Avonmouth	Rouen
	June 21st		
II	Divisional Ammunition Sub-Park	do.	do.
III	Motor Ambulances	do.	do.
	1st Day - June 21st		
IV	1/12th L.N.Lancs Reg (Pioneer Bn)	Southampton	Havre
V	2/13th London Regt	do.	do.
VI	2/14th ditto		
VII	2/5th London Bde R.F.A.		
VIII	H.Q. & 517 Co.Div.Train		
IX	H.Q. & No: 1 Sec.Div.Sig.Co.		
X	3/3rd London Field Co.R.E.		
	2nd Day June 22nd		
XI	Divisional Headquarters		
XII	Hd.Qrs. Divl.R.A.		
XIII	H.Q.179th Inf.Bde, Sec.Sig. Co. & 518th Co.Div.Train		
XIV	2/15th London Regt.		
XV	2/16th ditto		
XVI	2/8th London Bde R.F.A. (How)		
XVII	2/4th Field Co.R.E.		
XVIII	2/4th Field Ambulance		
XIX	2/5th ditto		
XX	2/2nd London Casualty Clg.Stn		
	3rd Day - June 23rd		
XXI	H.Q.180th Inf.Bde. Sec Sig. Co and 519th Co.Div.Train		
XXII	2/17th London Regt		
XXIII	2/18th ditto		
XXIV	2/19th ditto		
XXV	2/6th London Bde R.F.A.		
XXVI	H.Q.Divl.R.E.		
XXVII	1/6th London Field Coy.R.E.		
XXVIII	2/6th London Fd.Ambce.		
	4th Day - June 24th		
XXIX	2/20th London Regiment		
XXX	H.Q.181st Inf.Bde, Sec.Sig. Co. and 520.Coy Div.Train.		
XXXI	2/21st London Regiment		
XXXII	2/22nd ditto		
XXXIII	2/7th London Bde R.F.A.		
XXXIV	60th Divl.Cyclist Coy.		
XXXV	(H.Q.1/1st Hants Yeomanry) (Squadron 1/1st Hants Yeomanry)		
XXXVI	60th Mobile Veterinary Sec.		
XXXVII	60th Sanitary Section.		
XXXVIII	2/23rd London Regt.		
XXXIX	2/24th ditto.		
XL	Divisional Amm.Column.		

War Office, Q.M.G. 2
13.6.1916.

APPENDIX II a.

OVERSEAS MOVE

LOADING TIME-TABLE AND GROUPING - TUESDAY, June 20th to SATURDAY, June 24th inclusive - FRESH RATIONS

DATE	TIME	S.O. 179th Bde.	TIME	S.O. 180th Bde.	TIME	S.O. 181st Bde.	TIME	S.O. Dvl.Troops
TUES. June 20th	7.30 to 8.30	Pioneers ✠; 2/13✠; 2/14✠; B.H.Q.; 2/15; 2/16; 2/4 F.A.; 518 Co. A.S.C.	8.30 to 9.30	D.H.Q.; B.H.Q.; 2/17; 2/18; 2/19; 2/5 F.A.; 2/4 F.Co.R.E.; Cas.-C. Stn; 519 Co. A.S.C.	9.30 to 10.30	Signals ✠; 3/3 F.Co.R.E.✠ C.R.E.; B.H.Q.; 2/20; 2/21; 2/22; 2/23; 2/24; 2/6 F...; 1/6 F.Co.R.E.; Cyclists; 520 Co. A.S.C.	10.30 to 11.30	300 Bde.✠; 517 Co. A.S.C.; C...; 301; 302; 303; Yeo.; M.V.S.; D...C.
WEDY. June 21st	7.30 to 8.30	B.H.Q.✠; 2/15✠; 2/16✠; 2/4 F.A.✠; 518 Co. A.S.C.✠	8.30 to 9.30	D.H.Q.✠; 2/5 F.A.✠; 2/4 F.Co.R.E.✠; Cas. Clg.Stn.✠; B.H.Q.; 2/17; 2/18; 2/19; 519 Co. A.S.C.	9.30 to 10.30	C.R.E.; B.H.Q.; 2/20; 2/21; 2/22; 2/23; 2/24; 2/6 F...; 1/6 F.Co.R.E.; Cyclists; 520 Co. A.S.C.	10.30 to 11.30	C.R...✠; 303 Bde.✠ 301; 302; Yeomanry; M.V.S.; D...C.
THUR. June 22nd	-	Nil	8.0 to 9.0	B.H.Q.✠; 2/17✠; 2/18✠ 2/19✠; 519 Co. A.S.C. ✠	9.0 to 10.0	2/6 F.A.✠; 1/6 F.Co.R.E. C.R.E.✠; B.H.Q.; 2/20; 2/21; 2/22; 2/23; 2/24; Cyclists; 520 Co. A.S.C.	10.0 to 11.0	301 Bde.✠; 302 Bde.✠ Yeomanry; M.V.S.; D...C.
FRID. June 23rd	-	Nil	-	Nil	9.0 to 10.0	B.H.Q.✠; 2/20✠; 2/21✠; 2/22✠; Cyclists ✠; 520 Co. A.S.C.✠; 2/23; 2/24	10.0 to 11.0	302 Bde.✠; Yeo.✠; M.V.S.✠; D...C.
S.TY. June 24th	-	Nil	-	Nil	-	Nil	10.0 to 11.0	D...C.✠; 2/23✠; 2/24✠

(✠) Units drawing their last Fresh Ration.

APPENDIX II (4)

OVERSEAS RATIONS

DATE	TIE	S.O. 179th Bde.	TIE	S.O. 180th Bde.	TIE	S.O. 181st Bde.	TIE	S.O. Div. T's.
TUESDAY June 20th	3.0 to 4.0	Pioneers, 2/13, 2/14	–	Nil	2.0 to 3.0	(Signals, 3/3 F.Co. (R.E.	4.0 to 5.0	500 Bde. Base Details, 517 A.S.C.
WEDNESDAY June 21st	3.0 to 4.0	B.H.Q., 2/15, 2/16, 2/4 F.A., 518 A.S.C.	2.0 to 3.0	D.H.Q., 2/5 F.A., 2/4 F.Co. R.E., Casualty Clg. Station	–	Nil.	4.0 to 5.0	C.R.A., 303 Brigade.
THURSDAY June 22nd	–	Nil.	3.0 to 4.0	B.H.Q., 2/17, 2/18, 2/19, 519 A.S.C.	2.0 to 3.0	C.R.E., 2/6 F.A., 1/6 F. Co. R.E.	4.0 to 5.0	301 Brigade
FRIDAY June 23rd	–	Nil.	–	Nil.	3.0 to 4.0	B.H.Q., 2/20, 2/21 2/22, Cyclists, 520 A.S.C.	4.0 to 5.0	332 Brigade Yeomanry. H.V.S.
SATURDAY June 24th	–	Nil.	–	Nil.	–	Nil.	4.0 to 5.0	D.A.C., 2/23, 2/24

APPENDIX III

O.C. Headquarters Co.
60th. Divl. Train

    Refilling tomorrow Group "A" will take place at 8-30 a.m. at the same point as for to-day. Lorries arrive at dump at 7-30 a.m. The following Units are attached to your Group:-

        Divisional Headquarters
        No: 1 Sect. Signal Co.
        Headquarters Divl. Train
        303rd. Bde. R.F.A.
        2/17th. London Regt.
        2/5th. London Field Ambulance
        Headquarters Co. Divl. Train.

Train Headquarters,   Captain
25-6-16.   (sgd.) E.C. Seth-Smith Adjutant
                            60th. (London) Divisional Train

APPENDIX IV

Groups for refilling 27th.

"A" 517 Coy. A.S.C.
     300 Bde. R.F.A.
     301 " R.F.A.
     302 " R.F.A.
     303 " R.F.A.
     Det.3/3rd.Fd. Co. R.E.
     2/6th. London Fd.Amblce.
     2/4th. London Fd. Amblce.

R.P. on the Ternas Maizieres road. Head of R.P. at X roads 500 yards S.W. of "A" in Averdoingt.

"B" Bde. Hdqtrs.179th.Inf.Bde.
) 4 Battns.
     3/3rd. Fd. Co. R.E.
     Pioneer Battalion
     2/4th. Fd. Co. R.E.
     518 Co. A.S.C.

A C O.

"C" Divisional Headquarters
     Divl. Signal Co. No: 1 Sect
     Headqtrs. R.E.
     Headqtrs. R.A.
     Headqtrs. 180th. Inf.Bde.
) 4 Battns.
     519 Co. A.S.C.
     2/5th.London Fd.Amblce.
     1/6th. Fd. Co. R.E.

ST. POL - NUNCQ ROAD.

Head of refilling point 500 yards W. of "T" in Framecourt.

Lorries arrive and dump at 7 a.m.

Refilling to commence at 8-30 a.m.

APPENDIX V

SUPPLY GROUPING FOR REFILLING ON THE 28TH.

Group "A" Divisional Headquarters
    Hdqrs. R. E.
    " R. A.
    No. 1 Sec. Sig. Co.
    301st Bde: R.F.A.
    302nd do
    303rd do
    300th do
TINQUES. 2/4th Field Amblce.
    2/6th do
    Sec. 3/3rd Fd.Co.R.E.
    (in 60th Divl. area)
    Sec. 2/4th Fd.Co.R.E.
    (in 60th Divl. area)
    Hdqrs.Co. Divl. Train.
    Hdqrs. Divl. Train.

Group "B" Hqrs 179th Inf: Bde:
    2/13th Bn. London Regt.
    2/14th do
    2/15th do
    2/16th do
    Sec.of 3/3rd Fd.Co.R.E.
    (Details)(in 51st Divl. Area)
ACQ   Sec. 2/4th Fd.Co.R.E.(Details)
    (in 51st Divl. area)
    1/12th L.N.Lancs.Regt.
    (Pioneers)
    2/17th Bn. London Regt.
    2/18th do
    No. 2 Co. Divl. Train.

Group "C" Hdqrs.180th Inf:Bde:
    2/19th Bn.London Regt.
    2/20th do
TINQUES 1/6th Fd.Co R.E.
    No. 3 Co. Divl. Train.
    2/5th Fd. Ambulance

Group "D" Hdqrs. 181st Inf:Bde:
    No. 4 Co Divl. Train.
    2/21st Bn. London Regt.
TINQUES   2/22nd do
    2/23rd do
    2/24th do

POSITIONS OF REFILLING POINT - 28TH.

Group "A" - Group "C" - and Group "D".

On the PENIN - TINQUES Road, ½ mile South of the junction of the road with the ST POL - AUBIGNY Road. Refilling Point facing North.
All wagons will come on to the Refilling Point via the X-roads 600 yards North-East of the 2nd "N" in PENIN.

Group "B" ......---------------......A C Q .

TIME OF REFILLING.

Lorries dump 7 a.m.
Wagons to arrive 8.15 a.m. Refilling commences 8.30 a.m.

Units whose Supply Wagons are with them on the night of the 27/28th will send their wagons independently to the Refilling Points.

Instructions will be given at the Refilling Point as to whether Supply Wagons will remain with the Units on the night of the 28/29th, or return to the Headquarters of the Divisional Train Company of the Group to which the Unit is allotted.

FOR INFORMATION.

H.Q.60th Divn
27th June, 1916.

H.W.McCALL.
Major,
for D.A.Q.M.G.

7/5/1

ALC SUBJECT:-
Refilling Points,   **Appendix VI**

SUPPLY GROUPING FOR REFILLING ON THE 29TH.

Group "A"(1)
- Divisional Headquarters
- H.Q., R.E.
- H.Q., R.A.
- H.Q. & No. 1 Sec Sig. Co.
- Divl. Cyclist Coy.
- Sany. Section.
- Mob. Vet. Section.
- H.Q., Divl. Train.
- H.Q. Co. Divl. Train.
- 2/4th Fd. Amb. (less details with 51st Div.)
- Det. of 2/4th Fd. Co. in 60th Div. Area.
- Divl. Ammn. Col.

Group "A"(2).
- 303rd Bde. R.F.A.
- 3/3rd Fd. Co. R.E.
- 1/6th Fd. Co. R.E.
- 2/21st Ldn. Regt.
- 2/22nd Ldn. Regt.
- Det. of H.Q. Co. Div. Train (in 51st Div. Area)

Group "D".
- H.Q. 181st Inf. Bde.
- 2/23rd Ldn. Regt.
- 2/24th do.
- 302nd Bde. R.F.A.

Group "B".
- H.Q. 179th I. Bde.
- 2/13th Ldn. Regt.
- 2/14th do.
- 2/15th do.
- 2/16th do
- 2/17th do.
- 2/18th do.
- 1/12th L.N.Lancs Regt. (Pioneers)
- 300 Bde. R.F.A.
- 2/4th Fd. Co. R.E.
- No. 2 Co. Div. Train.

Group "C"
- H.Q. 180th I. Bde.
- 2/19th Ldn. Regt.
- 2/20th Ldn. Regt.
- 301st Bde. R.F.A.
- Det. of 1/6th Fd. Co. R.E. (in 60th Div. Area).
- 2/5th Fd. Amb. (less det. with 51st Div.)
- No. 3 Co. Div. Train.
- Det. of 3/3rd Fd. Co. R.E. (in 60th Div. Area.)
- /6th Fd. Amb. (less det. with 51st Div.)
- No. 4 Co. Div. Train.

POSITIONS OF REFILLING POINTS - 29TH.

Groups "A"(1), "C", and "D".
On the ST POL - ARRAS Road. Head of the refilling point due South of the "U" in TINCUES Facing East.

Groups "A"(2) and "B".
On the SAVY - ARRAS Road. Head of the refilling point one mile North of the "T" in LARRASSET.
(Ref. Map 11 (LENS) - 1/100,000.)

TIMES OF REFILLING.
Lorries dump at 7 a.m.
Refilling commences 8.30 a.m.

C. R. A.
C. R. E.
H.Q., 179th Infy. Bde.
H.Q., 180th Infy. Bde.
H.Q., 181st Infy. Bde.
O.C., Pioneer Battn.
O.C., Divl. Train, A.S.C.
A. D. M. S.
A. D. V. S.
Camp Commandant.
A. P. M.

For information.

H.Q., 60th Divn.
28th June 1916.

H. W. McCAIN.
Major,
for D.A.Q.M.G.

Confidential

War Diary

of

60TH (LONDON) DIVISIONAL, A.S.C. Train

From 1st July 1916 to 31st July 1916

VOLUME I No: 2

60

Vol 2

Walter Lucuth
Capt & Adjutant
60TH (LONDON) DIVISIONAL, A.S.C.

HAUTE AVESNES.
1/8/16

S.T/R/18

WAR DIARY or INTELLIGENCE SUMMARY

Army Form C. 2118

Place	Date	Hour	Summary of Events and Information	Remarks and references to Appendices
TINQUES	1/5		The Companies of the 60th Divisional train are located as follows:— Headquarters (No 1) Coy at TINQUES with detachment at SAVY. No 2 Coy — ACQ — No. 3 Coy. DOFFINE FARM near PENIN. — No 4 Coy CHELERS. The Division is now partly in the 51st area and partly in the 60th. Units in the 51st area are administered by the 51st Divisional Train all arrangements for transport and supplies are being carried out by no. There is not accommodation for the whole of No 1 (Hdqrs) Coy at SAVY Group A therefore has been split into A₁ and A₂ and the Group A₁ detachment of No 1 Coy. is in group A₂. Detachment of No 1 Coy is in group A₂. The detachment at SAVY consists of:— 1 Captain, 1 Transport Subaltern, the R.O. to act as S.O. 1 W.O. 1 H.T. Serjt. 1 H.T. Corporal 1 Res Cpl Groom 2 Saddlers 2 wheelers 4 spare drivers, 2 spare pairs of riders, and 6 horses. In all cases every the cooks and baggage wagons are return to the train Companies of their groups. For locales of units of the Division see appendix I.	App. I

WAR DIARY or INTELLIGENCE SUMMARY

Place	Date	Hour	Summary of Events and Information	Remarks and references to Appendices
TINQUES (Aplin)	1st		To dispose of units for supply purposes as shown in Appendix IV	App. IV
			The lines of descent and repletion as shown in Appendix III.	App. III
			Points of replenishments Nos 1, 3 and 4 Coys on the S. POL — ARRAS road rear of R.P. due S. of T in TINQUES. 1st Group A(H) — C. and D.T. No 2 Coy. 1st Group B. Replenish point few E. of ACQ on the ACQ — FREVIN — CAPELLE road. No 1 Coy (detachment) Group A(a) on the SAVY - ARRAS road head of the R.P. one mile N.W. of H in HAUTE- AVESNES.	
			All arrangements have worked satisfactorily and there is nothing unusual to report.	
			Wells and camps are good.	
			There are few trees in the area and the journeys from replenishing points to units do not in any case exceed 6 miles each way.	
			Supply wagons have had no difficulty in reaching their units.	

Map 11 LENS 1/100,000

Army Form C. 2118

WAR DIARY
or
INTELLIGENCE SUMMARY
(Erase heading not required.)

Instructions regarding War Diaries and Intelligence Summaries are contained in F.S. Regs., Part II. and the Staff Manual respectively. Title Pages will be prepared in manuscript.

Place	Date	Hour	Summary of Events and Information	Remarks and references to Appendices
TINQUES	2nd July.		There are no changes to report in the disposition of companies, groups, of units or times of reporting. The order was published to-day by General Headquarters to have transport renumbered with the new Certain units. This order will have to be worked on as later but transport will show when units require their own transport to remain with them.	
TINQUES	3rd July.		No change. Nothing unusual to record.	
	4th July.		No change. Nothing unusual to record.	
	5th July.		In connection with the P.P.O. the units have been regrouped as shown on Appendix IV. This has been done with a view to facilitating supply arrangements when to ensure the distances covered of transport collecting are easy.	Appx. IV

1875 Wt. W593/826 1,000,000 4/15 J.B.C. & A. A.D.S.S./Forms/C. 2118.

WAR DIARY
or
INTELLIGENCE SUMMARY
(Erase heading not required.)

Army Form C. 2118

Place	Date	Hour	Summary of Events and Information	Remarks and references to Appendices
TINQUES	6th		The following movements of Companies took place today.	
			No 1 (M/Gun) Coy. from TINQUES to SAVY.	
			Detachment - do - from SAVY to HAUTE-AVESNES.	
			No 3 Coy. ——— DOFFINE FARM to HAUTE AVESNES.	
			No changes in grouping have taken place.	
			Times of reveilly & descying as for the 5th.	
			There are no recurred exercises to record.	
			Movement of companies took place at 3 p.m.	
"	7th		The following are now the existing points:-	
			Group A (½) 100 yds of R.R. on the X roads 1 m. N.W. of H in HAUTE-AVESNES	
			Group B. W. of ACQ	
			Group C — ST. POL ARRAS road 1km of R.R. over Q in TINQUES N.W. of HAUTE-AVESNES	
			Group D — ST. POL ARRAS road " " due S. of Q in TINQUES	

WAR DIARY or INTELLIGENCE SUMMARY

Army Form C. 2118

Place	Date	Hour	Summary of Events and Information	Remarks and references to Appendices
TINQUES	8th	—	Units have now been re-grouped as shown in Appendix V. Times of repelief, parties & relieving points are as for the 7th. 2/Lieut Seligman, R.O. w. 2 Coy has been appointed purchasing officer for the Division.	
TINQUES	9th	—	Tours of relieving, parties & relieving points as for the 8th. There is nothing unusual to report. Instructions have been received from III Army to lend Establishment of Brit. Rail. an E.F wagons being withdrawn from all other companies and Coy pooled under O.C. No1 Coy.	

Army Form C. 2118

WAR DIARY
or
INTELLIGENCE SUMMARY
(Erase heading not required.)

Instructions regarding War Diaries and Intelligence Summaries are contained in F.S. Regs., Part II. and the Staff Manual respectively. Title Pages will be prepared in manuscript.

Place	Date	Hour	Summary of Events and Information	Remarks and references to Appendices
TINQUES.	10th		No change in existing arrangements to ensure efficient working of trains).	
"	11th		— do —	
	12th		— do —	
	13th		— do —	
	14th		Railhead moves from TINQUES to AUBIGNY. The following moves have taken place. Train Headquarters from TINQUES & HERMAVILLE SAVY to HAUTE-AVESNES. No 2. Coy — ACQ to HAUTE-AVESNES. " 3 " — HAUTE-AVESNES to ACQ. " 4 " — CHELERS to HAUTE AVESNES. Lieut MacDonigall O. No / Coy. takes on duties of Town Major HAUTE AVESNES. Regun OR No/ Coy 57th Divl Train.	

1875 Wt. W593/826 1,000,000 4/15 J.B.C. & A. A.D.S.S./Forms/C. 2118.

Army Form C. 2118

WAR DIARY
or
INTELLIGENCE SUMMARY
(Erase heading not required.)

Instructions regarding War Diaries and Intelligence Summaries are contained in F. S. Regs., Part II and the Staff Manual respectively. Title Pages will be prepared in manuscript.

Place	Date	Hour	Summary of Events and Information	Remarks and references to Appendices
TINTIGNIES	15th		The Division being now taken on the lines Companies are in their permanent position with the exception of No 2 coy. It is hoped that this coy. can be moved to HCQ in a few days. Units have been & grouped as shown in Appendix VI. Refilling points and lines of refilling as shown in Appendix VI. In order to meet existing conditions certain arrangements have been made for the disposal of baggage and E.F. wagons, and for finding additional transport for units. For orders published on this subject see Appendix VII. The position of units are as shown in attached VIII.	} Appx VI " VII " VIII
HERMALLE	16th		No change.	
	17th		The following units are added to Group A 25th and 26th A.A. batteries.	

1875 Wt. W593/826 1,000,000 4/15 J.B.C. & A. A.D.S.S./Forms/C. 2118.

Army Form C. 2118

WAR DIARY
or
INTELLIGENCE SUMMARY

(Erase heading not required.)

Place	Date	Hour	Summary of Events and Information	Remarks and references to Appendices
HERMAVILLE	17th	(contd.)	Approval is given of this XVII Corps for a reserve of 200 Reserves Zillots to be held at TILLOY for reinforcement Group. to charge.	
	18th		Changes of grouping of units as shown in Appendix VIII (a.) No 2 Coy moves from HAUTE AVESNES.	
	19th		Reliefs from Group A and D as per 18th. " " B " ACQ-ECOIVRES road from E PACQ. " " C " ACQ CAPELLE FERMONT road). Train headquarters moved from HERMAVILLE to HAUTE-AVESNES.	
	20th		Reliefs of Companies, repairing fronts and groupings of units unaltered. Nothing unusual to record.	

Army Form C. 2118

WAR DIARY
or
INTELLIGENCE SUMMARY
(Erase heading not required.)

Instructions regarding War Diaries and Intelligence Summaries are contained in F. S. Regs., Part II. and the Staff Manual respectively. Title Pages will be prepared in manuscript.

Place	Date	Hour	Summary of Events and Information	Remarks and references to Appendices
HAUTE AVESNES	21st		Nothing to record. No changes.	
	22nd		— do —	
	23rd		— do —	
	24th		35 - H.W. lines repaired 9.35 mules	
	25th		Order retiring from railhead unit have hereupon consecutive scheme and time table as shown in appendix IX. This scheme has been worked pretty satisfactorily. There has been no congestion at the railer, and the yard was cleared within 1 3/4 hours. Section arrived at Repellin generally approximately at following times.	

1875 Wt. W593/826 1,000,000 4/15 J.B.C. & A. A.D.S.S./Forms/C. 2118.

WAR DIARY
or
INTELLIGENCE SUMMARY
(Erase heading not required.)

Army Form C. 2118

Place	Date	Hour	Summary of Events and Information	Remarks and references to Appendices
HAUTE AVESNES	25.4	(Contd.)	Group D — at 12.30 p.m. " B — " 12.45 p.m. " A — " 1. p.m. " C — " 1.30 p.m. This allows time to water and feed horses after leaving AUBIGNY Station. Supplies as arranged and on protocols. The supply situation is now as follows:— West the event one day. Charges at R.P.s one day. Supply Column Empty. In the event of a sudden move being ordered, the supplies now on the ground will be packed up by the Supply Column of the Train and the Supply Column would join Lummis division at rail head.	

WAR DIARY
or
INTELLIGENCE SUMMARY

(Erase heading not required.)

Army Form C. 2118

Place	Date	Hour	Summary of Events and Information	Remarks and references to Appendices
HAUTE AVESNES	26"		All event arrangements as on for the 25". Received express from H.T. to reduce fresh quantity. Companies to dinner food meat being at their respective posts in addition to giving state already provided.	
"	27"		Nothing unusual to record. All arrangements working smoothly.	
"	28"		— do —	
"	29"		— do —	
"	30"		35. Bulls arrived from AUBIGNY Station in packing for 35. H.D.	
"	31"		Nothing unusual to record. All arrangements working smoothly.	

LIST OF UNITS OF THE 60TH DIVISION   APPENDIX I

1. Divisional Headquarters   VILLERS-CHATEL
2. Divl. Signal Company   "
3. ~~1/1st Hants Yeomanry~~
4. ~~Divl. Cyclist Company~~   "
5. H.Q. Royal Artillery

6. 300th Bde. R.F.A., A-Batty.)
                       B-   "   ) 179th Inf.Bde. area (with 51st Div.)
                       C-   "   )
                       D-   "   )

   301st   "   "   A-   "   )
                       B-   "   ) 180th Inf.Bde area.
                       C-   "   )
                       D-   "   )

   302nd   "   "   A-   "   )
                       B-   "   ) 181st Inf.Bde area.
                       C-   "   )
                       D-   "   )

   303rd "(How)"   A-   "   )
                       B-   "   ) Forward area (with 51st Div).
                       C-   "   )

7. Divl. Ammunition Column   - ST MICHEL-SUR-TERNOISE
8. H.Q. Royal Engineers   - VILLERS-CHATEL

9. 2/3rd London Field Co. R.E. - In 51st Div. area.
   2/4th   "   "   "   - In 51st Div. area.(with 179th Inf.Bde)
   1/6th   "   "   "   - In 51st Div. area.

10. H.Q. 179th Inf. Brigade   - ECOIVRES
    2/13th Bn. London Regt.)
    2/14th "   "   "   ) With 51st Division.
    2/15th "   "   "   )
    2/16th "   "   "   )
    M.G. Company, 179th Bde.   ditto.

11. H.Q. 180th Inf. Brigade   - PENIN
    2/17th Bn. London Regt.   - with 51st Div.
    2/18th "   "   "   - ditto.
    2/19th "   "   "   )
    2/20th "   "   "   ) - 180th Inf.Bde area.
    M.G. Company, 180th Bde.   ditto.

12. H.Q. 181st Inf. Brigade   - CHELERS
    2/21st Bn. London Regt.) - with 51st Division.
    2/22nd "   "   "   )
    2/23rd "   "   "   ) - 181st Brigade area.
    2/24th "   "   "   )
    M.G. Company, 181st Bde.   ditto.

13. Pioneer Bn. 1/12th N. Lancs - with 51st Division

14. H.Q. & 517 Coy., Divl. Train. - TINCQUES
              518   "   "   "   - ACQ
              519   "   "   "   - DOFFINE
              520   "   "   "   - CHELERS.

15. 2/4th London F. Ambulance   - 179th Brigade area
    2/5th   "   "   "   - 180th Brigade area
    2/6th   "   "   "   - 181st Brigade area

16. Divl. Sanitary Company   )
17. Mobile Veterinary Section) - VILLERS-CHATEL

Attached Units and Corps Troops.

ALC   SUBJECT:-
              Refilling Points.

Appendix II

SUPPLY GROUPING FOR REFILLING ON THE 29TH.

Group "A"(1)   Group "B".
   Divisional Headquarters   H.Q. 179th I. Bde.
   H.Q., R.E.   2/17th Ldn. Regt.
   H.Q., R.A.   VILLERS   2/14th do.
   H.Q. & No. 1 Sec Sig. Co.   CHATEL   2/15th do.
   Divl. Cyclist Coy.   2/16th do
   Sany. Section.   2/17th do.
   Mob. Vet. Section.   TINQUES   2/18th do.
   H.Q., Divl. Train.   1/12th L.N.Lancs Regt.
   H.Q. Co. Divl. Train.   (Pioneers)
   2/4th Fd. Amb. (less   300 Bde. R.F.A.
      details with 51st Div.) xxxxxxxxxxxxxxxxxxxxx
   Det. of 2/4th Fd. Co. in   xxxxxxxxxxxxxxx
      60th Div. Area.   2/4th Fd. Co. R.E.
   Divl. Ammn. Col. — ST. MICHEL SUR   No. 2 Co. Div. Train.
                               TERNOISE
Group "A"(2)   Group "C"
   303rd Bde. R.F.A. — FREVIN.CAPELLE   H.Q. 180th I. Bde.
   3/3rd Fd. Co. R.E. — MAROEUIL   2/19th Ldn. Regt.
   1/6th Fd. Co. R.E.   2/20th Ldn. Regt.
   2/21st Ldn. Regt.   301st Bde. R.F.A.
   2/22nd Ldn. Regt.   Det. of 1/6th Fd. Co. R.
   Det. of H.Q. Co. Div.   (in 60th Div. Area).
      Train (in 51st Div. Area)   1/6th Fd. Amb. (less det.
                                                      with 51st Div.)
                                              No. 3 Co. Div. Train.
Group "D".
   H.Q. 181st Inf. Bde.   Det. of 3/3rd Fd. Co. R.E.
   2/23rd Ldn. Regt.   (in 60th Div. Area.)
   2/24th do.   /6th Fd. Amb. (less det. with
   302nd Bde. R.F.A.   51st Div.)
                                              No. 4 Co. Div. Train.

POSITIONS OF REFILLING POINTS - 29TH.

Groups "A"(1), "C", and "D".
   On the ST POL - ARRAS Road. Head of the refilling point due South of the "U" in TINQUES Facing East.

Groups "A"(2) and "B".
   On the SAVY - ARRAS Road. Head of the refilling point one mile North of the "T" in LARRASSET.
   (Ref. Map 11 (LENS) - 1/100,000.)

TIME OF REFILLING.
Lorries dump at 7 a.m.
Refilling commences 8.30 a.m.

C. R. A.
C. R. E.
H.Q., 179th Infy. Bde.
H.Q., 180th Infy. Bde.
H.Q., 181st Infy. Bde.
O.C., Pioneer Battn.
O.C., Divl. Train, S.C.
A. D. M. S.
A. D. V. S.
Camp Commandant.
A. P. M.

Q/5/2

For information.

H. W. McCAIN.

H.Q., 60th Divn.   Major,
28th June 1916.   for D.A.Q.M.G.

APPENDIX III

REFILLING POINTS on 1st JULY 1916

Groups A.1. C and D. - On TINQUES - ARRAS road as for 30th June.

" B and A.2. at ACQ

    Times of Dumping :-

        A.1, C and D.....8.a.m.
        B and A.2........8.30.a.m.

    Times of Refilling:-

        A.1. C and D.....8.45.a.m.
        B................9.15.a.m.
        A.2..............10.30.a.m.

(sgd) H.G.SETH-SMITH.
Capt. &Adjt.for O.C.
60th (London) Div.Train

Train H.Q.
30-6-16.

APPENDIX IV

Grouping from and including the 5th July 1916 until further order.

Group A.

Divisional H.Q.
Divisional Signal Co.
H.Q. Royal Artillery.
300 Brigade R.F.A.
303 Brigade R.F.A.
H.Q. Royal Engineers.
H.Q.Co., Divl. Train.
2/5th Field Amb.
Mobile Vet. Section.

Group B.

2/3rd Field Co., R.E.
2/4th Field Co., R.E.
1/6th Field Co. R.E.(part)
H.Q. 179th Infty Brigade.
2/13th Battn.
2/14th Battn.
2/15th Battn.
2/16th Battn.
M.G. Co., 179th Bde.
2/17th Battn.
2/18th Battn.
2/19th Battn.(part).
M.G. Co., 180th Bde.
2/21st Battn.
2/22nd Battn.
M.G. Co., 181st Bde.
1/12th L.R. Lancs Battn.
No.2. Co., Divl. Train.
2/4th Field Amb.

Group C.

301st Bde. R.F.A.
Divl. Amm. Col.
1/6th Field Co., R.E.
H.Q. 180th Infty Bde.
2/19th Battn.(Part)
2/20th Battn.
H.Q. Divl. Train.
H.Q.Co.,Divl Train(detchmnt.)
No.3.Co., Divl. Train.
2/5th Field Amb.
Divl. Santy Coy.

Group. D.

302nd Bde. R.F.A.
H.Q. 181st Infty Bde.
2/23rd Battn.
2/24th Battn.
No.4.Co., Divl. Train.

APPENDIX V

To.

SUBJECT:- REFILLING POINTS.

C.R.A.
C.R.E.
H.Q. 179 Infy.Bde.   Q/5/9.
H.Q. 180   -do-
H.Q. 181   -do-
O.C. 60 Train.
A.D.M.S.
A.D.V.S.
S.S.O.
O.C. Pioneer Battn.
Camp Commandant.
A.P.M.
D.A.D.O.S.

The following detail regarding supplies is forwarded for your information and necessary action.

JULY 8th.

  Refilling points as for July 7th.
  Time of Refilling 8.30 a.m. for all groups.
  Time of Dumping 7.30 a.m. for all groups.

GROUPING FOR SUPPLIES.

  The Groups for July 8th will be as follows :-

GROUP "A".

Divisional Headquarters.
H.Q. & No.1 Sec. Signal Coy.
C.R.A.
301st Brigade R.F.A.
D.A.C.
C.R.E.
H.Q. Coy. Divl. Train (part)
2/6th Field Ambce.
Divl. Sanitary Sec.
Mobile Veterinary Section.

GROUP "B".

300th Brigade R.F.A.
1/6th Field Coy R.E. (Part)
179th Infy. Bde. H.Q.
2/13th, 2/14th, 2/15th, 2/16th Bns.
179th M.G. Company.
181st M.G. Company.
1/12th L.N. Lancs.
No.2 Coy. Divl. Train.
2/4th Field Ambce.

GROUP "C".

303rd Brigade R.F.A.
3/3rd Field Coy. R.E.
2/4th Field Coy, R.E.
2/17th Bn. London Regt.
2/19th & 2/20th Bns.
180th M.G. Company.
2/22nd, 2/23rd, 2/24th Bns.
No.3 Coy. Divl. Train.

GROUP "D".

302nd Brigade . R.F.A.
1/6th Field Coy R.E. (Part)
180th Infy.Bde. H.Q.
2/18th Bn. London Regt.
181st Bde. H.Q.
2/21st Bn. London Regt.
H.Q.Coy. Divl. Train (Part)
No.4 Coy, Divl. Train.
2/5th Field Ambce.
Salvage Company.

B. BARRETT.

H.Q. 60 DIVISION.
JULY 7th 1916.

Captain
D.A.Q.M.G.

AM

APPENDIX VI

SUBJECT:- REFILLING POINTS.

Q/5/9

C.R.A.
C.R.E.
H.Q. 179th Inf. Bde.
H.Q. 180th   do
H.Q. 181st   do
O.C. Pioneer Battn.
O.C. 60th Train.
A.D.M.S.
S.S.O.
Camp Commandant.
A.P.M.
D.A.D.O.S.
~~O/C SALVAGE CORPS~~

The following detail regarding supplies is forwarded for your information and necessary action.

JULY 15th.

Refilling points :- GROUPS A., B. and D. - ARRAS-ST.POL road, W. of HAUTE AVESNES.

GROUP C. - ACQ-ACOIVRES road E. of ACQ.

Time of Refilling 8 a.m.
Time of Dumping 6-30 a.m.

GROUPING FOR SUPPLIES.

The grouping for July 15th will be as follows :-

GROUP "A"

Divisional Headquarters.
C.R.A.
C.R.E.
Sanitary Section.
Mob. Vety. Section.
Train H.Q.
H.Q. & No.1 Sec. Signal Co.
303 Brigade R.F.A.
D.A.C.
No. 1 (H.Q.) Co. Div. Train
Medium T. M. Batteries.
XVIIth Corps Light Rly.
185 Tunnelling Co. R.E.
279   "   "
XVIIth Corps Cyclists
   ("A" Coy. & "C" Coy.)
Divisional Baths
Salvage Corps.
Hants Carabiniers.
21st Reserve Park.

GROUP "B".

Hqrs. 179 Inf. Brigade.
2/13, 2/14, 2/15, 2/16 Bns.
179 Bde. Machine Gun Co.
179th T. M. Battery.
3/3rd Field Company R.E.
2/4th Field Ambulance.
300 Brigade R.F.A.
1/12th L.N Lancs Regt.
No. 2 Coy. Div. Train.
60th Div. Cyclist Coy.

GROUP "C".

Hqrs. 180th Inf. Brigade.
2/17, 2/18, 2/19, 2/20 Bns.
180th Bde. Machine Gun Co.
180th T. M. Battery.
2/4th Field Company R.E.
2/5th Field Ambulance.
301 Brigade R.F.A.
No. 3 Coy. Div. Train.

GROUP "D".

Hqrs. 181st Inf. Brigade.
2/21, 2/22, 2/23, 2/24 Bns.
181st Bde. Machine Gun Coy.
181st T. M. Battery.

1/6th Field Company R.E.
2/6th Field Ambulance.
302nd Brigade R.F.A.
No. 4 Coy. Div. Train.

H.Q. 60th Divn.
14th July, 1916.

B. BARNETT.
Captain,
D. A. Q. M. G.

To O.C. 1, 2, 3, 4 Cos. and S.S.O.

ALLOTMENT OF WAGONS
(Provisional)

1. All Baggage and Supply Wagons will remain with the Divl. Train Companies with the following exceptions:-

  C.R.A. 1 Baggage Wagon and 1 Limber for Supplies.
  Each Inf. Bde Hdqrs. 1 Wagon for Baggage and Supplies.
  Each Art. Bde Hdqrs. --- ditto ---
  Divisional Hdqrs. 2 Baggage Wagons. 1 Supply Wagon.
  C.R.E. 1 Limber for Supplies and 1 Limber for Baggage.
  Pioneer Battalion. 2 Baggage Wagons without drivers or Horses.

2. Units requiring Transport for local work other than supplies will apply to the O.C. the Train Company of the Group to which they are allotted.

3. Supply Officers requiring extra Transport for Supplies, Green Forage, etc, will apply to the O.C. Train Coy. to which they are attached.

4. With reference to letter D. of T. No: 11313 dated 7-7-1916 all Wagons for Forage shewn in War Establishments Part VII are now on the establishment of the Headquarters Co. Div. Train, and are "pooled" under Divisional arrangements. These will be temporarily allotted as follows:-

  To each Battery of Artillery - 1 Wagon without Horses and Drivers.

  The remaining 5 Hay wagons remain with the O.C. No: 1 (Hdqrs) Coy, and are allotted as required by him.

5. As long as the Division is in occupation of the present sector of the Line, the Baggage Wagons of Artillery Units will be employed as required for the conveyance of Forage.

6. O.C. No: 1 (Hdqrs) Co. will allot daily one Limbered G.S. Wagon for Conveyance of Rations to detachment at Divisional Baths, MAROEUIL.

7. O.C. No: 2 Coy. will allot daily wagons for the Divisional Salvage Officer as required by him.

Train Headquarters,
In the field,
15th July 1916.
S.T./307/1.

        Captain
        Adjutant.
       60th Divisional Train

O.C. 1, 2, 3 and 4 Companies,
60th Divisional Train

    The attached copy of amended establishments, Divisional Train is forwarded for your information. In order to bring the Divisional Train Companies on to this new Establishment, the following adjustments will take place:-

1. Each of Nos. 2, 3 and 4 Cos. will hand over to No: 1 (Hdqrs) Co. the G.S. Wagon - complete turnout - allowed by War Establishments Part VII for extra Forage of a Brigade Headquarters.

2. O.C. No: 1 (Hdqrs) Co. will hand over 6 G.S. Wagons, as follows:-

    For Divisional Cyclist Co.....1 G.S. Wagon - Baggage
                             .....1 G.S. Wagon - Supplies.

    For Headquarters of Yeomanry
      Regiment ....1 G.S. Wagon for Baggage & Supplies.

    For A Squadron Hants Carabineers......................1 G.S. Wagon for Baggage
                         ....2 G.S. Wagons for Supplies

    Instructions as to the Unit to which these are to be handed over will be issued later.

3. O.C. No: 1 (Hdqrs) Co. will exchange one Limbered G.S. Wagon now allotted for Supplies of the Divisional Signal Coy, for one G.S. Wagon.

4. No: 1 (Hdqrs) Co. will then have 20 G.S. Wagons for extra Forage.

5. For temporary allotment of Wagons, see this office No:S.T./307/1 of to-days date.

Train Headquarters,
15th July 1916.
S.T./307.

                                        (sgd) H.Glethsmith Captain
                                                   Adjutant
                                             60th Divisional Train

COPY.

D.D.S. & T. III Army.

D.of T.
No:11313.

In consequence of recent changes in the composition of a Division, the number of Draught Horses and vehicles in a Divisional Train has altered materially from the Establishment, as given on pages 81 and 82 of War Establishments Part VII.

A revised transport table has been drawn up showing the
    Vehicles
    H.D.Horses
    Drivers (for vehicles and spare Draught Horses)
there now should be in a Divisional Train. The number of motor Cars is subject to a local deduction of two cars.

Sufficient copies for you to distribute to those concerned are enclosed and it is requested that when circulating the table instructions may be given for Divisional Trains to conform forthwith to this table in all respects.

        (sgd) J.H.YOUNG. Col. for Brig-Gen.
                 Director of Transport.

G.H.Q.
7-7-1916.

COPY.

WAR ESTABLISHMENT
A DIVISIONAL TRAIN
Transport (ii)

DETAIL	H.Q. & H.Q.Co.			Three Coys			TOTAL			Remarks
	Vehicles	H.D. Horses	Drivers	Vehicles	H.D. Horses	Drivers	Vehicles	H.D. Horses	Drivers	
Bicycles (for Field Post Office	1	-	-	-	-	-	1	-	-	(a)
" Inter-commn	2	-	-	-	-	-	2	-	-	Will be driven
" Req.& Supply details	7	-	-	21	-	-	28	-	-	and horsed
Cart Maltese for Med.Equipt.	1	1	-	-	-	-	1	1	-	by spare dri-
Wagon GS for Postal Service.	1	2	1	-	-	-	1	2	1	vers and spare
Wagon Limb.GS for Tech.Eqpt.	1	2	1	3	6	3	4	8	4	horses of the
Carts, Water	1	2	1	3	6	3	4	8	4	Train
Wagons (for Baggage	2	4	2	6	12	6	8	16	8	
G.S. (for Cooks	2	4	2	6	12	6	8	16	8	
Wagons (G.S.	3(a)	-	-	-	-	-	3	-	-	
Spare (Limbd.G.S.	2(a)	-	-	-	-	-	2	-	-	
Spare Draught Horses		20	10	-	12	6	-	32	16	
Motor Cars	2	-	-	3	-	-	5	-	-	
BAGGAGE SECTION										(b)
Wagon Lbd.GS for HQ Divl.Engrs.	1	2	1	-	-	-	1	2	1	For a Division
(for Divl.H.Q.	2	4	2	-	-	-	2	4	2	with 16-4.5"
(" HQ Divl.Arty.	1	2	1	-	-	-	1	2	1	Howitzers, add
(" 3 F.A.Bdes(Composite)	15	30	15	-	-	-	15	30	15	to both the
Wagons(" 1 F.A.Bde (b)	4	8	4	-	-	-	4	8	4	Baggage and
(" Div.Ammn Col.	5	10	5	-	-	-	5	10	5	Supply Sectns:
G.S. (" H.Q.3 Inf.Bdes.	-	-	-	3	6	3	3	6	3	1 GS Wagon
(" 12 Inf.Battns.	-	-	-	24	48	24	24	48	24	2 HD Horses
(" 1 Pioneer Battn)	2	4	2	-	-	-	2	4	2	1 Driver
SUPPLY SECTION										
Wagons (for Divl.H.Q.	1	2	1	-	-	-	1	2	1	(c)
Limbd.(" H.Q.Div.Arty	1	2	1	-	-	-	1	2	1	To be used as
G.S. (" H.Q.Div.Engrs	1	2	1	-	-	-	1	2	1	a Pool for the
(" H.Q.3 Inf.Bdes	-	-	-	3	6	3	3	6	3	carriage and
										distribution of
("3 F.A.Bdes(Composite)	12	24	12	-	-	-	12	24	12	extra forage for
("1 F.A.Bde (b)	3	6	3	-	-	-	3	6	3	all Units in
(" Div.Ammn Col.	5	10	5	-	-	-	5	10	5	the Divn. as
(" 3 Fd.Coys.R.E.	3	6	3	-	-	-	3	6	3	required.
(" Signal Coy.R.E.	1	2	1	-	-	-	1	2	1	
Wagons(" 12 Inf.Battns.	-	-	-	24	48	24	24	48	24	
(" 1 Pioneer Battn.	2	4	2	-	-	-	2	4	2	
G.S. (" 3 Fd.Amblces.	3	6	3	-	-	-	3	6	3	
(" Mob.Vet.Sect.	1	2	1	-	-	-	1	2	1	
(" 3 M/Gun Coys.	-	-	-	3	6	3	3	6	3	
(" Extra Forage (c)	20	40	20	-	-	-	20	40	20	
TOTAL	108	201	100	99	162	81	207	363	181	

SECRET   60th Division   APPENDIX VIII

LOCATION RETURN

UNIT	LOCATION
H.Q. 60th Division	HERMAVILLE
H.Q. R.A.	HERMAVILLE
A.B.300	LARESSET
C.D.300	ACQ
A.B.C.301	LARESSET
A.B.C.D.302	ACQ
A.B.D.303	CAPELLE FERMONT
C.303	ACQ
D.A.C.	FREVENT CAPELLE
H.Q. R.E.	HERMAVILLE
2/4th Field Co.	MAROEUIL
3/3rd do.	ANZIN
1/6th do.	MONT ST. ELOY
Signal Co.	HERMAVILLE
179th Inf. Bde)	CENTOR SECTOR
179th M.G. Co.)	CENTRE SECTOR
180th Inf. Bde)	LEFT SECTOR
180th M.G. Co.)	LEFT SECTOR
181st Inf. Bde)	RIGHT SECTOR
181st M.G. Co.)	RIGHT SECTOR
Pioneer Battalion	LOUEZ
H.Q. Divl. Train A.S.C.	HAUTE AVESNES
517th Coy.	HAUTE AVESNES
518th do.	ACQ
519th do.	ACQ
520th do.	HAUTE AVESNES
A.D.M.S.	HERMAVILLE
4th Field Amb.	ECOIVRES
5th do.	HAUTE AVESNES
6th do.	HAUTE AVESNES
Sanitary Sect.	HERMAVILLE
Mobile Vet. Section	MAISON ROUGE

APPENDIX VIIIa

BH.

SUBJECT:- SUPPLIES.

H.Q. XVII Corps.
C.R.A.
C.R.E.
H.Q. 179th Infy.Bde.
H.Q. 180th -do-
H.Q. 181st -do-
O.C. Pioneer Bn.
O.C. 60th Train.
A.D.M.S.
S.S.O.
Camp Commandant.
A.P.M.
D.A.D.O.S.

A.P.S.
A.D.V.S.
D.S.C.
O. i/c Baths, MAROEUIL.
O.C. 60th Cyclist Coy.
O.C. 185th Tunnelling Co.R.E.
O.C. 290th Rly. Coy, R.E.
O.C. Mobile Vet. Sec.
O.S. Salvage Corps.
O.C. 62nd A.A. Battery.

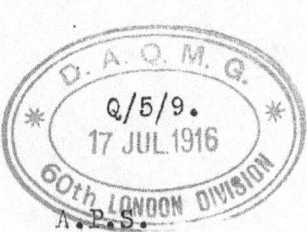

Q/5/9.
17 JUL 1916
D.A.Q.M.G.
60th LONDON DIVISION

....

The following detail regarding supplies is forwarded for your information and necessary action.

JULY 18th.

GROUP "A"   Delete: Y and Z Medium Trench Mortar Batteries.
             Divisional Headquarters.
             Add:-
                    Anti-Aircraft Battery.
             62nd   "   "   "
             1/12th L.N. Lancs Regt.

GROUP "B".   Delete:- 3/3rd Field Coy, R.E.
                       1/12th L.N. Lancs Regt.
             Add:-   2/4th Field Coy, R.E.
                       X Medium Trench Mortar Battery.

GROUP "C".   Delete:- 2/4th Field Coy, R.E.

             Add:-   1/6th Field Coy, R.E.
                       Y Medium Trench Mortar Battery.

GROUP "D".   Delete:- 1/6th Field Coy, R.E.

             Add:-   Divisional Headquarters.
                       3/3rd Field Coy, R.E.
                       Z Medium Trench Mortar Battery.

Time and place of REFILLING and DUMPING

as for the 16th instant.

....

"Q"
JULY 17th 1916.

Captain
D.A.Q.M.G.

APPENDIX IX
259/4

To O.C. 1,2,3,4, Coys. 60th. Div. Train.

The following is the scheme for the working of the Transport for Units' supplies daily from Railhead to Refilling Point.

(1). The scheme will come into force on the 24th. inst.
2. Table A. shews the present distribution of the baggage wagons.
3. Table B. shews composition of supply sections working from Railhead to Refilling Point. Footnote to be carefully noted by Supply Officers.
4. All arrangements for additional transport should any be required from the reserve park or D.A.C. also notification as to times convoys should arrive at the Station etc., will be made from this office.
5. From the 24th. inst. inclusive the extra Forage wagons now with Artillery Batteries will be sent daily to the refilling point to draw forage.
6. From the 23rd, inst, all demands for Transport by Units will be submitted through this office.
7. The following officers will be in command of sections A.B. and D.
        Section "A"........2/Lieut. Dumas.
        do. "B"........Lieut. Randall.
        do. "D"........2/Lieut. Redwood.
Lieut. Wornum will proceed with section "C" to the Station and will work in conjunction with the R.T.O. ensuring that the wagons of section "C" (provided by the D.A.C.) are brought into the Station yard in the correct order etc.,.
8. Section "B" will be collected on the Capelle-Fermont --- Acq road, ½ mile W. of Acq.   section
9. The A.S.C. officer with each wagon will be responsible that each wagon is told off for its correct load before arriving at the Station. This must be worked out from the loading table which is to be made by the supply officers concerned.
10. Table "C" gives the time table for the arrival of the sections at the station.
11. All officers detailed for this duty will reconnoitre the station yard at Aubigny before the morning of the 24th. O.C. companies will report to this office that they have done so.
12. The section of the 21st. Reserve Park which will supply the transport is situated at Agnieres, - ½ mile E. of the C. in Capelle-Fermont. Ref. Map 11. Lens. 1/100,000.
Lieut. Dumas and Lieut. Redwood, will proceed with their wagons of the 60th. Divl. Train to this point daily and will there pick up the wagons of the 21st. Reserve Park.
13. D.A.C. wagons proceed independently to the station and will be met there by Lieut. Wornum.

22-7-16.
S.T./259/4.

(Sgd) H.G. Lech Smith Capt.
Adjt.
60th. (London) Divisional Train.

DISTRIBUTION OF BAGGAGE WAGONS.

Table A.

No. of Company	Available with Companies	(a) Required daily for supplies from Railhead	(b) Permanently Allotted	(c) Available for other work
No: 1 H.Q. Co.	12	6		6
No: 2 Co.	14	8		6
No: 3 Co.	13	8		5
No: 4 Co.	14	5	R.E. Stores Maroeuil 3 (x)	6
	(5	27	3	23

(x) Commencing on 26th.

These figures are necessarily variable and only form a guide.

COMPOSITION OF SUPPLY SECTIONS WORKING FROM RAILHEAD

Table "B"

Group A.	Group B.	Group C.	Group D.
Baggage Wagons of No. 1 Company......6	Baggage Wagons of:- No. 2 Coy..........8) No. 3 Coy..........8)	D.A.C....20	Reserve Park....20
Reserve Park......25	No. 4 Coy..........5)		

Should any Group require additional wagons for drawing Supplies from Railhead, the Company Commander will detail them from the wagons shewn under heading (c) on table A.

Table "C"

Section D   9.30.a.m.
Section B   9.45.a.m.
Section C   10.0.a.m.
Section A   10.15.a.m.

Vol III

Confidential

War Diary
— of —
60th London Divl Train

From 1st August 1916 to 31st August 1916

Volume I   No 3

ST/R/18
1.9.16

Army Form C. 2118.

Sheet 1

August 1916

60TH (LONDON) DIVISIONAL, A.S.C.

WAR DIARY or INTELLIGENCE SUMMARY
(Erase heading not required.)

Place	Date	Hour	Summary of Events and Information	Remarks and references to Appendices
HAUTE AVESNES	1st	—	General situation in regard to Co's. Brit. Train is as follows:— Train Headquarters TRY FARM HAUTE AVESNES. No 1. (Westgarth's Coy) — HAUTE AVESNES — No 2 Coy. ACQ. No 3 Coy. ACQ — No 4 Coy. HAUTE AVESNES. Refilling Points — Groups A and D on the ARRAS – ST. POL road, W. of the R.P. on the X roads due N. of 3.g E in HAUTE AVESNES. (Ref. Map Sheet 11 LENS 1/100,000) Group B in the ACQ – ECOIVRES road just E of ACQ. Group C on the road running N.W. from the road junction 500 yds. N.E. of last E in FREVIN-CAPELLE to the O of CAPELLE FERMONT. Refilling points are satisfactory. Coss Shelters have been erected. Each during being provided with a supply table, grocery store, meat cloth and shop shelter.	

WAR DIARY
or
INTELLIGENCE SUMMARY

Army Form C. 2118.
SHEET 2
TRAIN

August 1916.
60TH (LONDON) DIVISIONAL, A.S.C.

Place	Date	Hour	Summary of Events and Information	Remarks and references to Appendices
			Times of refilling are as follows:-	
			Group D - 8 a.m. - Group B and C. - 8.30 a.m. - Group A - 9 a.m.	
			Refillers for each group takes from 3/4 hour to an hour.	
			The units of this Division are located as shown in Appendix I.	
			The grouping of units for supply purposes is as shown in appendix II	
			The sources of the supply columns have now been dispensed with supplies being drawn direct from railheads by horse transport.	
			This transport is drawn (a) from Wagon wagons of Train	
			(b) from 2/1st Reserve Park	
			(c) from D.T.C	
			The organization of these reliefs and orders as to their working are as shown in APPENDIX III	

WAR DIARY or INTELLIGENCE SUMMARY

Army Form C. 2118.
Sheet 3

Place	Date	Hour	Summary of Events and Information	Remarks and references to Appendices
HAUTE AVESNES.	3rd		Enemy shelled neighbourhood of ACQ between hours of 10.30 p.m. and 11.15 p.m. mostly with 4.13 c.m. gun mounted on the railway. About 32 shells were sent over about 10% of which were blind. No damage was done. Nos. 2 and 3 Coys. moved their lines from the neighbourhood of ACQ. No. 2 proceeding N about 3/4 mile in the direction of CAMBLAIN L'ABBÉ, No. 3 W. as far as CAPELLE FERMONT. The horses of the 1st Indian Cavalry B.T.C. stampeded through the lines of No. 3 Coy carrying them to Travrege. But but all were recovered by 8 a.m. Two men were injured. About 2 a.m. O. Train gave orders for supplies to be removed from present dumps to ARRAS - ST. POL road in rear of group A. R.P.	

Army Form C. 2118.
Sheet 4

WAR DIARY
or
INTELLIGENCE SUMMARY

August 1916

60TH (LONDON) DIVISIONAL TRAIN.

(Erase heading not required)

Place	Date	Hour	Summary of Events and Information	Remarks and references to Appendices
HAUTE AVESNES.	3rd	(Contin)	All supplies were at the rendezvous by 4.45 a.m. and various returned to the Company lines at ACQ.	
- " -	4th		Refilling points for all groups on the ST. POL — ARRAS road. Group D — 8 a.m. Groups A.B.C. — 9 a.m. Times of refilling.	
			The supply section working from railhead dumped supplies for all groups on the ARRAS — ST. POL road.	
- " -	5th		Refilling points and times of refilling as for the 4th. Supply section working from railhead dumped supplies for groups B and C on the ARRAS — ST POL road. Groups at ACQ.	

WAR DIARY or INTELLIGENCE SUMMARY

Army Form C. 2118. Sheet 5

60TH (LONDON) DIVISIONAL TRAIN

August 1916

Place	Date	Hour	Summary of Events and Information	Remarks and references to Appendices
HAUTE AVESNES	6th	—	All repairs, paints and tents preparing on to the 14th the events of interest in comparison to traces.	
"	9th	—	Instructions received from Div. Headquarters to complete rations in supplementary points to the following scale:— MAISON BLANCHE — 1400 preserves. ZIVY — 200 — BENTATA — 200 — NEUVILLE ST. VAAST — 14,000 preserves and 6,800 Iron. ECURIE — 1400 preserves. 1400 preserves rations invoiced at ECURIE. Instructions received from Div. Headquarters to split trains of iron rations at NEUVILLE-ST.-VAAST and to store 3,400 at that place and remaining 3,400 in dug outs at ECURIE.	
"	11th	—	Owing to mishap on the line, Pack Train did not arrive until 1:30 p.m. Tracopoi sections are packed in neighbourhood of	

Army Form C. 2118.
Sheet 6

WAR DIARY
or
INTELLIGENCE SUMMARY
(Erase heading not required.)

60TH (LONDON) DIVISIONAL, A.S.C. TRAIN.

August 1916.

Place	Date	Hour	Summary of Events and Information	Remarks and references to Appendices
HAUTE AVESNES.	11th (Contd.)		At AUBIGNY to await arrival of Pack Train. Train at entrheas began unloading at dumps between 4 p.m. and 5 p.m. Train was only 25% frozen. was arrived remainder being preserved meat. 39%. 7 Men arrived remainder being to cover bacon, jam and milk than to group D. from the P.S.O. arranges to complete from N°7 Field Depot PREVENT.	
	14th.		The organisation of Transport convoys supplies from railheas to refilling point has been reorganized. The reorganization effects a saving of 20 wagons daily. The services of the D.A.C being thus dispensed with. The scheme is shewn in the attached appendices IV, and V. and VI. & VII. Appendix I also shews the system under which the Transport of the Train is at present working.	

2449 Wt. W14957/M90 750,000 1/16 J.B.C. & A. Forms/C.2118/12.

WAR DIARY
or
INTELLIGENCE SUMMARY

(Erase heading not required.)

Army Form C. 2118.

Place	Date	Hour	Summary of Events and Information	Remarks and references to Appendices
HAUTE AVESNES.	16th		2,400 men taken and invalided at ECURIE.	
	20th		Evacuation of 1400 prisoners Patients at MAISON BLANCHE. The Pack Train arrived late at Railhead. Loading at railhead commenced at 10.50 a.m. Completed 12.40 p.m.	
	22nd		Evacuation completed at 2.1vs of 200 prisoners patients " " BENTATA. 200 " " NEVILLE ST. VAAST of 1400 walking Prisoners	
	23rd		Patients and 3400 Iron Rations.	
	31st		There are no further points of interest to record during the preceding month. All Camp and Transport arrangements	

Army Form C. 2118.

Sheet 8

WAR DIARY
or
INTELLIGENCE SUMMARY

60TH (LONDON DIVISIONAL. TRAIN.
(Erase heading not required)

Instructions regarding War Diaries and Intelligence
Summaries are contained in F. S. Regs., Part II.
and the Staff Manual respectively. Title Pages
will be prepared in manuscript.

Place	Date	Hour	Summary of Events and Information	Remarks and references to Appendices

have worked smoothly.

The weather with the exception of the last three days has been fine.

On the 30th it was found necessary to ship two lines (Headquarters & Coys and some wagon from Yeis on b roads on account of the heavy rains.

The Divisional Train is complete in personnel and transport with the exception of 2 H.D. horses and 1 rider.

There has been considerable difficulty in keeping the Ech. Group wagons + vans to the artillery in a circd. of repair but No 1 Coy has been got an wheeled repairs up to date.

Army Form C. 2118.

Sheet 9.

WAR DIARY
or
INTELLIGENCE SUMMARY

(Erase heading not required.)

60TH (LONDON) DIVISIONAL ~~A.S.C.~~ TRAIN

August 1916

Place	Date	Hour	Summary of Events and Information	Remarks and references to Appendices
HAUTE AVESNES	31/8		~~Supplies~~ as had ~~~~ to events of ~~Hostilities~~. No events of interest to record. A short report of the purchasing officer for given troops is attached in appendix VIII. A short report of purchasing officer for fresh vegetables is attached in appendix IX. The units remuneration scheme is now in hand and the scheme as put forward by Brig. Nelyn of Ales to Train is shewn in APPENDIX	

In The Field.
1/9/16

M.W. Kennish
Capt. & A.D.S.T.

60TH (LONDON) DIVISIONAL ~~A.S.C.~~ TRAIN

War Diary August 1916
60 London Div'l Train

Appendix I

List of Locations of Units

Right Sector

181st Inf. Bde. HQ.	Etrun	
Adv: HQ	G.9.b.2.9.	
Res. Btn.	Etrun	
Right Art. Group HQ	G.9.b.2.9.	
Batteries A.301	Wagon Lines Larosset	
B.301	do	
C.301	do	
B.300	do	
A.300	do	
D.256	do	
B.258	Trevin Capelle	
2/3rd Field Co. R.E. HQ	Anzin	
1 Co. Pioneers	Anzin & Louez.	

Centre Sector

179th Inf. Bde HQ	Ecoivres	
Adv: HQ	A.8.d.7.5.	
Res. Btn	Bray.	
Centre Art. Group HQ	Madagascar	
Batteries A.258	Wagon Lines etc	Trevin Capelle
A.302		Acq
B.302		do
C.302		do
D.302		do
D.260		Haute Avesnes
C.303		Acq
C.300		do
2/4th Field Co. R.E.		Maroeuil
1 Co. Pioneers		Ariane

Left Sector

180th Inf. Bde. HQ	Mont St Eloy.	
Adv. HQ	A.8.C.7.9.	
Res. Btn	Mont St. Eloy.	
Left Art: Group HQ	Berthonval	
Batteries C.258	Wagon Lines etc.	Trevin Capelle
A.303		Capelle Fermont
B.303		do
D.303		do
A.260		Haute Avesnes
B.260		do
C.260		do
D.300		Acq
1/6 Fd. Co. R.E.		Mont. St Eloy
1 Co Pioneers		Neuville St Vaast
HQ Pioneers and 1 Co.		Maroeuil

War Diary August 1916   Appendix II
60 (London) Div¹ Train

Groups for the 18th July 1916

Group A.

C.R.A.
C.R.E.
Sanitary Section
Hd. No¹. [Necleg] Co
303 Bde R.F.A.
D.A.C.
No. 1 (HQ) Co Div Train
17th Corps Light Rly
185 Tunnelling Co R.E.
2/9   "   "   "
17th Corps Cyclists
  ('A' Co & 'C' Co)
Divisional Baths
Salvage Corps
Haute Carabiniers
21st Reserve Park
Anti-Aircraft Battery
62nd A.A. Battery
1/12th L.N. Lancs (Pion)

Group "B"

Hqrs 179 Inf Bde
2/13, 2/14, 2/15, 2/16 Btns
179 Bde M G Co
179 T.M. Battery
2/4 Fd Amblce
300 Bde R.F.A.
No 2 Co. Div Train
60 Div Cyclist Co
2/4th Field Co R.E.
1/4 Co R.E.

Group C

Hqrs 180 Inf Bde
2/17, 2/18, 2/19, 2/20 Bns
180. Bde M G Co
180 T.M. Battery
2/5th Field Amblce
301 Bde R.F.A.
No 3 Co Div Train
1/6 Fd Co R.E.

Group D

Hqrs 181 Inf Bde.   2/21, 2/22, 2/23, 2/24 Bns
181 Bde M G Co.   181 T.M Battery
2/6th Fd Amblce   302 Bde R.F.A
No 4 Co Div Train   Div¹ Hdqrs
3/3 Fd Co R.E.   X, Y, + Z Med: T.M Batteries
Train HQ

Refilling Points Groups A & D - Arras-St Pol road W. of
                                  Haute Avesnes
         Group C - Acq. Ecouivres Road E of Acq
Time of Refilling D.- 8.0. C & B. 8.30. A. 9.0
         Time of Dumping - 6.30.

WAR DIARY   AUGUST 1916.   Appendix III
60th. (London) Divisional Train.

To O.C. 1,2,3,4, Coys. 60th. Div. Train.

The following is the scheme for the working of the Transport for Units' supplies daily from Railhead to Refilling Point.

(1). The scheme will come into force on the 24th. inst.
2. Table A. shews the present distribution of the baggage wagons.
3. Table B. shews composition of supply sections working from Railhead to Refilling Point. Footnote to be carefully noted by Supply Officers.
4. All arrangements for additional transport should any be required from the reserve park or D.A.C. also notification of times as to times convoys should arrive at the Station etc., will be made from this office
5. From the 24th. inst. inclusive the extra Forage wagons now with Artillery Batteries will be sent daily to the refilling point to draw forage.
6. From the 23rd. inst. all demands for Transport by Units will be submitted through this office.
7. The following following officers will be in command of sections A.B. and D.

      Section "A"......2/Lieut. Dumas.
      do.   "B"...... Lieut. Randall.
      do.   "D"......2/Lieut. Redwood.

Lieut. Wornum will proceed with section "C" to the Station and will work in conjunction with the R.T.O. ensuring that the wagons of section "C" (provided by the D.A.C.) are brought into the Station yard in the correct order etc.,.
8. Section "B" will be collected on the Capelle-Ferment ---Acq road, ½ mile W. of Acq.
9. The A.S.C. officer with each section will be responsible that each wagon is told off for its correct load before arriving at the Station.
This must be worked out from the loading table which is to be made by the supply officers concerned.
10. Table "C" gives the time table for the arrival of the sections at the Station.
11. All officers detailed for this duty will reconnoitre the station yard at Aubigny before the morning of the 24th. O.C. companies will report to this office that they have done so.
12. The section of the 21st. Reserve Park which will supply the transport is situated at Agnieres,- ½ mile E. of the C. in Capelle-Fermint. Ref. Map 11 Lens. 1/100,000.
Lieut. Dumas and Lieut. Redwood, will proceed with their wagons of the 60th. Divl. Train to this point daily and will there pick up the wagons of the 21st. Reserve Park.
13. D.A.C. wagons proceed independently to the station and will be met there by Lieut. Wornum.

            (Sgd) H.G.Seth-Smith Capt.
                  &
22-7-16.   Adjt.
S.T./259/4.   60th. (LONDON)Divisional Train.

S.F. Wagons No 1 Coy.

        R.A.........15
        Battns...... 2
        181st.Bde... 2
        Lent to No 2.1

COMPOSITION OF SUPPLY SECTIONS WORKING FROM RAILHEAD

Table "B"

Group A.	Group B.	Group C.	Group D.
Baggage Wagons of No.1 Company......8	Baggage Wagons of:- No. 2 Coy.........6) No. 3 Coy.........6)	D.A.C.....20	Reserve Park....18
Reserve Park.....22	No. 4 Coy.........4)		

    Should any Group require additional wagons for drawing Supplies from Railhead, the Company Commander will detail them from the wagons shewn under heading (c) on table A.

Table "C"

        Section D.........9.30.a.m.
        Scetion B.........9.45.a.m.
        Section C........10.0 .a.m.
        Section A........10.15.a.m.

WAR DIARY Aug. 1916.   60th London Div. Train   APPENDIX IV

O.C. 1.2.3.4 Co. Gd Train.   O.C. 21st Reserve Park
O.C. D.A.C.   Headquarters 60th Division "Q"

From Friday 18th inst inclusive, Transport Sections working from Railhead to Refilling Point will be composed as follows:—

No. 1 Section — Group A
    Supply Wagons 300 Bde R.F.A. — 4
    Supply Wagons. D.A.C. — 5
    Cooks Wagon No. 1 Co Div Train — 2
    21st Reserve Park — 18
                                                  29

No. 2 Section — Group B
    Baggage Wagons 4 Battns 179 Inf. Bde — 8
    Supply Wagons 302 Bde R.F.A. — 3
    Cooks Wagons No 2 Co: Div Train — 2
    21st Reserve Park — 6
                                                  19

No 3 Section Group C
    Baggage Wagons 4 Battns - 180 Inf. Bde — 8
    Supply Wagons 302 Bde R.F.A. — 4
    Cooks Wagons No 3 Co Div Train — 2
    21st Reserve Park — 6
                                                  20

No 4 Section Group D
    Baggage Wagons 4 Battns - 181 Inf. Bde — 8
    Supply Wagons 301 Bde R.F.A — 4
    Cooks Wagons No 4 Co Div Train — 2
    21st Reserve Park — 6
                                                  20

Times of arrival of Sections at Aubigny will be as follows:—
    Group D. 9.30am
           A   9.30am
           B. 9.45 am
           C. 10. am

O.C. Sections will arrange direct with O.C. Section 21st Reserve Park at Aquieres the time at which they will pick up the Reserve Pk Wagons.

All Wagons arriving at Aubigny Station must be clearly marked with the letter of the Group to which they belong.

A Divisional Routine Order is being published this day giving amended Grouping of Units and Times of Refilling. The attention of all Company Officers is called to this order.

Train HR.
16.8.16.
S.T/259/27

(sd) H.G. Seth-Smith Captain
                          Adjutant
                       60th Div Train

WAR DIARY   AUGUST 1916.
60th. (London) Divisional Train

Appendix V

Urgent

HEADQUARTERS
60th. DIVISION

    Herewith statements shewing working of the Transport of the 4 Companies of the Train.

Train Headquarters
21-8-16.
S.T./259/28.

Colonel
Commanding
60th.(London) Divl. Train.

HEADQUARTERS COMPANY - GROUP "A".

Transport State, week ending 19/8/1916.

Units composing Group	Vehicles per Establt.		How working.			
	Mark X	L.G.S.	A. To Unit with Supplies No. / Time of refilling.	B. To Aubigny	C. Permanently with Units.	D. In the pool
H.Q. of Company:-						
Cooks	2		2 / 9 a.m.			
Baggage	2				2	2
Technical		1			1	
Postal	1				1	
Extra Forage	20				20 (x)	
Spare vehicles	3 ∅	2				
						6
Supply Section:-						
C.R.A.		1	1 / 9 a.m.		1	
C.R.E.		1	1 / 9 a.m.			
M.V.S.	1		1 / 9 a.m.			
Sig.Coy.	1		1 / 9 a.m.			
300 R.F.A.	4		4 / 1 p.m.	4 x		
D.A.C.	5		5 / 1 p.m.	5 x		
Hants. Yeo.	1		9 a.m.		1	
Pioneer Btn.	2		2 / 9 a.m.			
D.H.Q.		1	No. 4 Coy.			
Baggage Section:-						
D.H.Q.	1		No. 4 Coy.			
C.R.A.	1		Out of order.			1
C.R.E.		1			1	
300 R.F.A.	5				1	4
D.A.C.	5		3 Hay 9 a.m.			2
Hants. Yeo.	1				1	
Pioneer Btn.	2			2		

x These vehicles go to Aubigny in the morning,
   and also to units with rations in the afternoon.

PERMANENT TRANSPORT FATIGUES

1 G.S. Wagon to Maroeuil
1 G.S. Wagon   Haute Avesnes
1 L.G.S. Company Lines, fatigue
1 G.S. Wagon to No: 64, Hermaville
1 G.S. Wagon, Water fatigue.
2 G.S. Wagons permanently with Convalescent Camp at Hermaville

∅ 2 Lent to O.i/c Baths at Maroeuil

(x) 15 With R.A.   )
    3 With Infy. Bdes.   )
    3 Permanently under repair.)

No: 2 Company 60th. Divl. Train   Group "B"

Transport State, week ending 19-8-16.

Units composing Group	Vehicles per Estabt.		How working			
	Mk. X	L.G.S.	A. To Unit with Supplies No: Time of Refill'g	B. To Aubigny	C. Permanently with Units	D. In the Pool

H.Q. of Company

				-x-		
Cooks	2	-	2	1.30.p.m.	2	-	-
Baggage	2	-	-	--	-	2	-
Technical	-	1	-	--	-	1	-

Supply Section

179. Bde. H.Q.	-	1	1	8.30.a.m.	-	-	-
4 Battalions	8	-	8	8.30.a.m.	-	-	-
179 M.G.Co.	1	-	1	8.30.a.m.	-	-	-
2/4th. F,Amb.	1	-	1	8.30.a.m.	-	-	-
2/4th. Fd. Co. R.E.	1	-	1	8.30.a.m.	-	-	-
303rd.Bde. R.F.A.	4	-	4ø	1.30.p.m.	4ø	-	-

Baggage Section

179. Bde.H.Q.	1	-	-	--	-	1	-
4 Battalions	8	-	-	--	8	-	-
303rd.Bde.R.F.A.	5	-	-	--	-	1	4

-x- To Aubigny in the morning and to the Units with Supplies in the afternoon.

ø 4 Wagons go to Aubigny in the morning and to Units with Supplies in the afternoon.

PERMANENT TRANSPORT FATIGUES

Town Major.................................2 Wagons
2/4th. R.E. Supplies.......................1 Extra wagon
Trench Mortar B.H.Supplies................1 Wagon
Manure....................................1 Wagon
Ordnance Stores...........................1 Wagon

In addition every two days.....1 wagon goes for vegetables
                               1 wagon goes for R.E. Stores,etc.

No: 3 Company. 60th. Divl. Train

Transport State, week ending 19-8-16.   Group "C"

Units composing Group	Vehicles per Estab.		How working			
	Mk.X	L.G.S.	A — To Unit with Supplies	B — To Aubigny	C — Permantly with units	D — In the Pool
			No:	Time of Refill'g		
H.Q. of Company						
Cooks	2	-	2	1.30.p.m. @	2	-
Baggage	2	-	-	--	-	2
Technical	-	1	-	--	-	1
Supply Section						
180.Bde.H.Q.	-	1	1	8.30a.m.	-	-
4 Battalions	8	-	8	8.30a.m.	-	-
180.M.G.Co.	1	-	1	8.30a.m.	-	-
2/5th. F.Amb.	1	-	1	8.30a.m.	-	-
1/6th.Fd.Co.R.E.	1	-	1	8.30a.m.	-	-
302.Bde.R.F.A.	4	-	4 @	1.30p.m.	4 @	-
Baggage Section						
180.Bde H.Q.	1	-	-	--	-	1
4 Battalions	8	-	-	--	8	-
302.Bde.R.F.A.	5	-	-	--	-	1	4

@ These Vehicles go to Aubigny in the morning and to the Units with Supplies in the afternoon.

The following work is done daily by No: 3 Company from wagons under Heading "D" and by working those under heading "A" double journeys:-

Town Major.........................1 Wagon
Bde.H.Q.-Ordnance and Canteen......1 Wagon.

No: 4 Company, 60th. Divl. Train   Group "D"

Transport State, week ending 19-8-16.

Units composing Group	Vehicles per Estab. Mk.X	Vehicles per Estab. L.G.S.	How working A To Unit with Supplies No: Time of Refill'g		How working B To Aubigny	How working C Permantly with Units	How working D In the Pool

H.Q. of Company

Cooks	2	-	2	1.30p.m.	2 @@	-	-
Baggage	2	-	-	--	-	2	-
Technical	-	1	1	--	-	1	-

Supply Section

181.Bde.H.Q.	-	1	1	8.30.a.m.	-	-	-
4 Battalions	8	-	8	8.30.a.m.	-	-	-
181.M.G.Co.	1	-	1	8.30.a.m.	-	-	-
2/6th.Fd.Amb.	1	-	1	8.30.a.m.	-	-	-
3/3rd.Fd.Co.R.E.	1	-	1	8.30.a.m.	-	-	-
301 Bde.R.F.A.	3	-	3@@	1.30.p.m.	3 @@	-	-

Baggage Section

181.Bde.H.Q.	1	-	-	--	-	1	-
4 Battalions	8	-	-	--	8	-	-
301.Bde.R.F.A.	4	-	-	--	-	1	3

@@ These Wagons go to Aubigny in the morning and to Units with Supplies in the afternoon.

PERMANENT TRANSPORT FATIGUES

1 Limber (Technical) with Supply Details daily.

1 G.S. Wagon (Baggage) to D.A.D.O.S. daily.

War Diary
60th London Div⁶ Train.   Aug: 1916   APPENDIX VI

Subject:- Supplies.

                                                    QS/9
                                              16. Aug 1916.

O.C. 60ᵗʰ Train.

     The following alterations in the Grouping of Units
will take place as from Friday 18ᵗʰ August, inclusive.

         300ᵗʰ Brigade R.F.A. from Group "B" to Group "A"
         303ʳᵈ   ———————————   "A"   "B"
         301ˢᵗ   ———————————   "C"   "D"
         302ⁿᵈ   ———————————   "D"   "C"

     As from the 18ᵗʰ instant inclusive the following
Units will refill at 1 p.m. instead of 8.30. a.m.

     300. 301. 302. 303 Bdes R.F.A. & D.A.C.
     Nos. 1.2.3.4 Coys Divisional Train.

     The four Artillery Brigades will continue to
draw their Hay at 8.30. am.

                                    (Sd) B. Barrett.
                                         Captain
"P"   D.A.Q.M.G.
August 16ᵗʰ 1916

War Diary August 1916   APPENDIX VII
60th London Divisional Train

O.C. 1. 2. 3. 4. Cos. 60 Div Train

From tomorrow inclusive until further orders the time of arrival of Sections at Aubigny Station will be as follows:-

  Group D. ——— 9.30. am
  ——— A ——— 9.30 am
  ——— B ——— 9.45 am
  ——— C ——— 10. am

After loading at the Station, Transport will not water &c at Aubigny but will go straight through to the dumps.

(1) Working party detailed to off-load will parade at "D" Dump at 10.45 am and not at 11.30 am

(2) Loaders arriving on Group "A" wagons must be sent to Group "D" dump to help offload as soon as possible.

(3) S.O. No. 4 Co must send the working party to Group A dump directly Group "D" is offloaded.

    (sd). J.G. Leth-Smith
      Capt. Adjt
    60 London Div Train

ST/205/76
14 Aug. 1916

WAR DIARY - APPENDIX IX VIII

Report of purchases made during month of August 1916.

The purchases come under the following headings :-
    (1) Green Forage
    (2) Oatstraw
    (3) Quick Lime
    (4) Medical Comforts

(1). Total spent 5927 fr. Amount of kilos bought 258,800. This averages a price of 2.33 francs per 100 kilos, which contracts favourably with the Army maximum price of 5.00 fr. per 100 kilos. Also according to the allowance of 12 centimes per day per horse, I should be entitled to spend, roughly about 27000 fr. during the month, instead of actually 5927 fr. I have endeavoured to satisfy as far as possible the requirements of the Units, by buying them fields as near as possible to their own horse lines and also in certain cases I have managed to get the farmers to cut the field themselves, but during the latter weeks this has become more and more difficult, as the farmers have needed all their labourers for bringing the harvest.

(2). I have purchased 1550 kilos of oatstraw in all at 6 fr. per 100 kilos. This has been used for binding round the box of the wheels in accordance with Third Army Orders.

(3). I have purchased 1550 kilos of quick lime, at 1.50 fr. per 100 kilos, the Army maximum price being 3.00 fr. This has been used for whitewashing and disinfectant purposes.

(4). I have purchased

    (a) Milk
    (b) Eggs
    (c) Fish
    (d) Cabbage
    (e) Cauliflower
    (f) Carrots

As required by the Field Ambulances (d)(e)(f) were only purchased during the earlier period: Subsequently all purchases of vegetables were taken over by 2/Lieut. Henley. The Eggs varied in price from 20-25 centimes, This is slightly in excess of the Army rate, but eggs are rather scarce; and the difficulty of obtaining them suddenly to meet unexpected requirements is obvious.

General Observations.

I have found the farmers in the district, without exception, pleasant and moderate in their charges. Especially in the purchase of Green forage, they have sold at a low rate-partly of course because they cannot find the labour themselves. I should like especially to mention M. Dupont of Etrun, a very large owner of land, from whom I have made many purchases. He has shown me every courtesy and has been of the greatest possible assistance to me in every way. I am glad to say that, with one exception, no forage has been cut by mistake from a field not bought by me: and the difficulty in France, where there are no hedges to mark the boundary, of clearly showing a field, is considerable. I have endeavoured to overcome this difficulty by a liberal use of notices "To the Green Forage Field".

                                      (Sgd) V.J.Seligman 2/Lt
                                        Divl. Purchasing Office
                                        60th. Division.

Appendix IX.

Vegetables bought for 60th. Division during the month of August 1916. by Q.293. 60th. Divisional Train

In consequence of an order issued at the beginning of the month to the effect that green vegetables were to be purchased to supplement the 6 oz ration per man per day, which comes up from railhead.

I got into touch with Mdme Dekeyzer of St. Pol and have thus been able to issue 2 ounces of fresh vegetables to every man each day.

My purchases during the present month (Aug) comprised 35024 kilos and made up of Cabbages, Carrots, and Turnips.

All three of these commodities are very popular and I have been able to buy carrots at 5 francs per 100 kilos below the fixed price.

Cabbages and Turnips have been bought at the Govt. price and I am endeavouring to procure the former at a slightly cheaper rate now that the supply is becoming more plentiful.

I do not buy Cabbages in very large quantities as (1) the price is higher than either Carrots or Turnips and (2) the Q.M's tell me that it is difficult to get them up to the trenches owing to the space they take up.

```
Cabbages are bought at 20 francs per 100 kilos. (Govt. price 20)
Carrots    "    "   "  16   "     "    "    "   (  "     "   21)
Turnips    "    "   "  10   "     "    "    "   (  "     "   10)
```

The merchant tells me that all three of these articles are fetching higher prices now but I think she will allow me to keep the original prices (vide above).

The system of delivering the goods is as follows.

The vegetables come up to Aubigny Station in bulk in a truck.

I meet the merchant at the station and load the 4 G.S. wagons for groups A.B.C.D. and a lorry which takes vegetables for the D.S.C.

I get her man to unload the truck and load the wagons, thereby checking the amount.

The carrots are made up into bottes of 15 kilos apiece.
The Turnips "   "   "   "   "   " 10   "   "
The Cabbages at present average 2 kilos each.

I select bottes of both turnips and carrots and weigh them first to ensure full weight. I have invariably found this to be correct.

The same applies to the cabbages, but owing to the impossibility of packing them in bottes I average them from selections made.

After each wagon is loaded I total the exact amount of each vegetable (my figures are previously made out from 3316's) and give the driver a waybill which he hands to the Supply Officer before unloading.

I then total the days issue- show it to the merchant and pay her through my imprest account.

I have always had every reason to believe she is perfectly honest and this assumption has been fully corroborated by the Mayor of Aubigny.

This issue is made twice a week - on Monday and Thursdays so that I draw 3 and 4 days supplies at a time respectively.

(Sgd) F.A.H. Henley, 2/lieut.
R.O. 180th. Infantry Brigade.

Confidential

Vol 4

WAR DIARY OF

60th LONDON DIVISIONAL TRAIN

From 1st September 1916 To 30th September 1916

VOLUME ~~X~~ No: 4.

S.T/R/18
1st October 1916.
In The Field

WAR DIARY
or
INTELLIGENCE SUMMARY

Army Form C. 2118.
Page I

60TH (LONDON) DIVISIONAL ~~A.S.C.~~ TRAIN.

September 1916

Place	Date	Hour	Summary of Events and Information	Remarks and references to Appendices
HAUTE AVESNES	1st	—	Location of Companies. On the 1st September the locations of the Divisional Train Companies are as follows:—	
			No 1 (Headquarters) Coy. -- HAUTE AVESNES. E 22 d. 5. 5" sheet 51 C.	
			No 2 Coy. -- -- ACQ -- -- E 12 c. 1.1 Sheet 51 C	
			No 3 Coy. -- -- ACQ -- -- E 11 d 5". 3 -- do --	
			No 4 Coy. -- -- HAUTE - AVESNES. -- E 28 a 9.9. Sheet 51 C.	
			Supply Refilling Points. No 1 Coy. GROUP A.	E 21 b. 3.5" to E 21 b 7.3.
			No 2 Coy. GROUP B.	E 18 b. 9. 9.
			No 3 Coy GROUP C.	E 11 Central.
			No 4 Coy. GROUP D.	E 21 b 7.3 to E 22 a 2. 2.

Army Form C. 2118.
Page #2

WAR DIARY
INTELLIGENCE SUMMARY
60TH (LONDON) DIVISIONAL TRAIN

September 1916

Place	Date	Hour	Summary of Events and Information	Remarks and references to Appendices
HAUTE AVESNES (contd)	1st		For location of units of the Division see Appendix I	App. I
			For grouping of units for supply purposes see Appendix II	App. II
			The system All supplies are at present being brought from railhead (AUBIGNY) to dumps by Horse Transport.	
			For composition of dumps see Appendix III Two of railheads working from railhead at railhead Group D 9.30 a.m Group A 9.30 a.m Group B 9.45 a.m App III Group C 10 a.m Came into operation on 18th August.	App. III
			This present system has been working satisfactorily.	
			Times of repletion Groups B and D — 8.30 a.m Group C and A — 8.45 a.m.	
			All rations supply wagons proceed direct to units and return independently to Company lines.	
			Working of Transport App. IV shews the system under which been working to at present working.	App. IV

Army Form C. 2118.
Page 3

WAR DIARY
or
INTELLIGENCE SUMMARY

(Erase heading not required.) 60TH (LONDON) DIVISIONAL. S.C. TRAIN

September

Place	Date	Hour	Summary of Events and Information	Remarks and references to Appendices
HAUTE AVESNES	1st		Reserve of Supplies. Received instructions to withdraw 300 tins tobacco from ECURIE and to withdraw 300 tins tobacco from NEUVILLE ST VAAST and nineteen them in the ELBE SHELTERS.	
"	2nd		No change b'rend.	
"	3rd		Refilling at railhead. Today took place at the following times. Groups B and A. - 8.30 a.m. " B - 8.45 a.m. " C - 9 a.m. All transport clear of the station by 9.45 a.m. Reserve of Supplies. 600 tins tobacco were installed in the ELBE SHELTERS.	
"	7th		Transport. The following allocation has been made in the allotment of 21st Reserve Park wagons working from railhead. No.1 Section Group A wagons of 19 wagons - 12 " B. C. & D. wagons of 7 ewt - 9.	

2449 Wt. W14957/Mgo 750,000 1/16 J.B.C. & A. Forms/C.2118/12.

September Page 4 Army Form C. 2118.

WAR DIARY
or
INTELLIGENCE SUMMARY 60TH (LONDON) DIVISIONAL TRAIN

Place	Date	Hour	Summary of Events and Information	Remarks and references to Appendices
HAUTE AVESNES.	11th		Supplies 4th South Staffs Regt. arrived in the Divl. area. = Transport lines located at BRAY. and attached for rations to Group B. O.C. Train inspected 1st Line. Transport of 180th Inf. Bde. Condition of Transport on the whole very satisfactory. Transport Ref. appx. II Wago Coy permanent Transport fatigues. The two wagons permanently attached to Convalescent Camp at HERMAVILLE are withdrawn today. O/c Convalescent Camp so stated to Antonin all demands for transport as required to this office.	
	12th		Movement of Coy. No 3 Coy. moves today from ACQ to HAUTE AVESNES, and co located at E.28.b 7.7 sheet 57c. Location of new supply dumps at E.21.a 2.9 sheet 57c. No change in grouping of units for supplies is at present made necessary by this move.	

2449 Wt. W14957/M90 750,000 1/16 J.B.C. & A. Forms/C.2118/12.

WAR DIARY or INTELLIGENCE SUMMARY

Army Form C. 2118.
Page 5

60TH (LONDON) DIVISIONAL TRAIN

September

Place	Date	Hour	Summary of Events and Information	Remarks and references to Appendices
HAUTE AVESNES	13		Antoine: 200 W. Coy., R.E. arrived in Divisional Area, and is located at BRAY and attached for rations to GROUP B. Transport: Evolution to report. Supplies: Trains of drawing from rail head. "B" 9.15 a.m. "C" 9.30 a.m. "A" 9.45 a.m. "D" 10 a.m.	
"	14		From 17th Batt. Kings Liverpool Regt. arrived in Div. area and is located at ECOIVRES and attached for supplies to GROUP B. X and & 3º Div. T.M. Battys arrived and attached for rations to Group B. Transport: O.C. Train inspected 1st Line Transport of 1/12 L.N. Lancs (Pioneer) Battalion. Also Ex Echelon of Transport on the whole satisfactory. Working Party of 40 men for Corseyeri T.M. Ammunition for 180 Ind. Whole Forces of Ind. Train.	

WAR DIARY or INTELLIGENCE SUMMARY

Army Form C. 2118.
Page 6

P (47/74) (LONDON) DIVISIONAL A.E. TRAIN

September 1916

Place	Date	Hour	Summary of Events and Information	Remarks and references to Appendices
HAUTE AVESNES	15		Supplies. 176 Tunnelling Coy. arrived in Divl area and is attached for rations to Group C. Information received at 12 midnight that following units will leave AUBIGNY STATION 9 a.m. tomorrow. 1st Dorset Regt. 17th Northumberland Fusiliers, 206 Fd. Coy. R.E. X & Y 30 Div. T.M. Batteries. O.C. No 2 Coy instructed to turn necessary Transport to take supplies to such at 6 a.m. and necessary arrangements made accordingly.	
	16		Times of units as above performed his trans.	
	17		Times of units as above took places. Taupin O. Trans full below instruction as to inspection of Ledien Transport. App. V	V

WAR DIARY

September 1916

INTELLIGENCE SUMMARY

Army Form C. 2118. Page 2

TRAIN, 60TH (LONDON) DIVISIONAL, A.S.C.

Place	Date	Hour	Summary of Events and Information	Remarks and references to Appendices
HAUTE AVESNES	18	—	Instructions received from Divl. Headquarters at 5.30 p.m. to run train to Infantry, R.E. and R.F.A. 150 pounds of man Crickets of the Supply Column from the F.S. depot. Train arrives D dump 10.15 p.m. Leave of train completed at 2.30 a.m.	
	19.		Following units left Divl. area. 17 Kings Liverpool Regt. 1/11 Sonic Surrey Regt., 2nd Fd. Coy. R.E. relieves up to and inclusive 20".	
	20"		Following units left Divl. area. 1st Dorsets Regt. 17". Londinensians Fusiliers 1 206 Fd. Coy. R.E.	
	21."		No other change in order of units, regrouping of coins of event purposes has been made Vide A.P.O VI reach effect from 23rd.	VI

WAR DIARY

September 1916   TRAIN

of 60TH (LONDON) DIVISIONAL. A.S.C.

INTELLIGENCE SUMMARY

Army Form C. 2118.   Page 8

Place	Date	Hour	Summary of Events and Information	Remarks and references to Appendices
HAUTE AVESNES.	27.		An exercise scheme of Transport working from railhead to Brigade area took place today and has worked satisfactorily. The details of this scheme are set forth in App. VII. The point of loadings amounts to 12 wagons daily. Rations is divided into two, as shown in app. VIII. The wagons used for the 2nd. regiment also bring up supplies for rations according to time table. The Transport tables as shown in App. IV are also corrected. The bearers will as rendered . 9 companies daily is amended and this each shown in app. VIII will in future be rendered.	VII

Army Form C. 2118.

WAR DIARY of 60TH (LONDON) DIVISIONAL TRAIN

INTELLIGENCE SUMMARY

September 1916

Page 2

Place	Date	Hour	Summary of Events and Information	Remarks and references to Appendices
HAUTE AVESNES	29.		Transport Wagons 179 - 180 - 181 2nd line have been notified that the two Coys who this an arrchment 3 wagons daily to keep 1st line Transport well stock Transport	
			Ration 179 2nd line will demand their feed Or No 2 Coy.	
			Extract of General Remarks During the month good progress has been made in preparation of wanti accoutrement. No 4 coy horse lines rugs and shelter are complete. Transport of 1, 2, & 3 coys nearly Complete. Average daily no. of sick horses during the month has been 26 for the Train. Average sick men 12.	
	30.			

September 1916

TRAIN.
WAR DIARY
or
INTELLIGENCE SUMMARY

Army Form C. 2118.
Page 10

Place	Date	Hour	Summary of Events and Information	Remarks and references to Appendices
			General Remarks Continued	
			No complaints have been received during the month of the non arrival or late arrival of rations & hangers.	
			All arrangements have worked smoothly.	
			The weather on the whole has been good.	
			From 6 to 10 wagons daily have been sent to several farmers to help get in the harvest.	
			Appendices II and III are reports of purchasing officers for green forage and vegetables on the work done during the month.	

A. H. Rees
[signature]
Cap. & O.C.
TRAIN.

80TH (LONDON) DIVISIONAL TRAIN.
1/10/16

WAR DIARY
60 London Div Train
SEPTEMBER 1916

APPENDIX I

LIST OF LOCATIONS OF UNITS :

Right Sector.
    181st. Inf.Bde.H.Q.   Etrun
            Adv.H.Q.   G.9.b.2.9.
            Res.Btn.   Etrun

    Right Art.Group H.Q.   G.9.b.2.9.
        Batteries A.301   Wagon lines Laresset
              B.301   do.
              C.301   do.
              B.300   do.
              A.300   do.
              D.256   do.
              B.258   Frevin Capelle
    3/3rd.Field Co. R.E.H.Q.   Anzin
    1.Co. Pioneers.   Anzin & Louez

Centre Sector.
    179th. Inf.Bde.H.Q.   Ecoivres.
            Adv.H.Q.   A.8.d.2.5.
            Res.Btn.   Bray.
    Centre Art.Group.H.Q.   Madagascar
        Batteries A.258   Wagon lines etc., Frevin Capelle.
              A.302   ACQ.)
              B.302   do.)
              C.302   do.)
              D.302   do.)
              D.260   Haute Avesnes.
              C.303   ACQ.
              C.300   do.
    2/4th.Field Co.R.E.   Maroeuil
    1.Co. Pioneers   Arians.

Left Sector.
    180th. Inf.Bde.H.Q.   Mont St.Eloy
            Adv.H.Q.   A.8.c.7.9.
            Res.Btn.   Mont St.Eloy.
    Left Art.Group H.Q.   Berthonval.
        Batteries C.258   Wagon lines etc., Frevin Capelle.
              A.303   Capelle Fermont
              B.303   do.
              D.303   do.
              A.260   Haute Avesnes
              B.260   do.
              C.260   do.
              D.300   ACQ
    1/6th. Field Co. R.E.   Mont St.Eloy.
    1.Co. Pioneers.   Neuville St.Vaast

    H.Q. Pioneers & 1 Co.   Maroeuil.

War Diary
60th London Div Train
September 1916.   APPENDIX II

Grouping of Units – 1.9.16

Group A
CRA
CRE
Sanitary Section
Mobile Vet Sec
Signal Co RE
HQ DAC
DAC
185 Co RE
278 Co RE
Div Baths
Salvage Co
Reserve Park
Pioneer Bn
19 Cps Light Rly
40 AA Battery
Anti Gas School
517 Co ASC

Group B
179 Bde HQ
2/13, 2/14, 2/15, 2/16
Lons Lond: Regt
179 M.G. Co
179. T.M.B
147. A.S.C. RE
2/4 Fd Ambulce
2/4 Fd Co RE
N. 60. T. M Batty
303 Bde RFA HQ
A, B+D Batts +C Batty
578 Co ASC
Town Major Exoirres

Group C
2/17, 2/18, 2/19
+ 2/20 Lons L Regt
3/5 Fd Amblce
180 M G Co
180 T.M. Batty
180. Bde HQrs
1/6 Fd Co RE
302 Bde RFA HQ
A.B.C.D Battys "
No 3 Co ASC

Group D
HQ 60 Div
60 Convalescent Co
HQ 301 RFA
B.C.D Battys "
3/3 Fd Co RE
HQ 181 Bde

2/21 2/22 2/23 + 2/24
Lons L. Regt
181 M G Co
181 T.M. Batty
XYZ Med T.M Batts
18th Bn Cheshire Regt

No 4 Co ASC
2/6 Fd Ambulance
HQ Div Train

War Diary - Co London Div Train
September 1916

APPENDIX III

O.C. 1.2.3 & 4 Cos Co Train. S.S.O. O.C. 21st Res Pk
O.C. D.A.C.   H.Q. Co Div Q

From Friday 15th inclusive, Transport Sections working from Railhead to Refilling Point will be composed as follows:-

No: 1 Section - Group A

Supply Wagons 300 Bde R.F.A.	4
Supply Wagons D.A.C.	5
Cooks Wagons No 1 Co Div Train	2
21st Reserve Park	18
	29

No: 2 Section - Group B

Baggage Wagons - 4 Battns 179 Inf Bde	8
Supply Wagons 303 Bde R.F.A.	3
Cooks Wagons No 2 Co Div Train	2
21st Reserve Pk.	6
	19

No 3 Section - Group C

Baggage Wagons 4 Bttns 180 Inf Bde	8
Supply Wagons 302 Bde R.F.A.	4
Cooks Wagons No 3 Co Div Train	2
21st Reserve Park	6
	20

No 4 Section Group D

Baggage Wagons 4 Battns - 181 Inf Bde	8
Supply Wagons 301 Bde R.F.A.	4
Cooks Wagons No 4 Co Div Train	2
21st Reserve Park	6
	20

Times of arrival of Sections at AUBIGNY will be as follows.
Group D - 9.30 am   Group A 9.30 am
Group B - 9.45 am   Group C 10. am

O.C. Sections will arrange direct with O.C. Section 21st Res. Pk at AGNIERES, the time at which they will pick up the Res. Pk. Wagons.

All Wagons arriving at Aubigny Station must be clearly marked with the letter of the Group to which they belong.

A Divl Routine Order is being published this day giving amended programs of Units & times of Refilling. The attention of all Coy Officers is called to this order.

(sd) K.G. Seth-Smith Captain
Adjutant
Co Div Train

Transptd 57/759/27
16K.

- WAR DIARY -
60th. (London) DIVISIONAL TRAIN. September 1916.
HEADQUARTERS COMPANY - GROUP "A".

Appendix IV.

Transport State, week ending 19/8/16.

Units composing Group	Vehicles per Estabt.		How working.			
			A. To Unit with Supplies	B. To Aubigny.	C. Permanently with Units.	D. In the pool.
	Mark X	L.G.S.	No. Time of refilling.			
H.Q. of Company:-						
Cooks	2		2 9 a.m.			
Baggage	2				2	2
Technical		1			1	
Postal	1				1	
Extra Forage	20				20 (x)	
Spare Vehicles	3 ∅≠	2				
Supply Section:-						
C.R.A.		1	9 a.m.		1	
C.R.E.		1	1 9 a.m.			
M.V.S.	1		1 9 a.m.			
Sig. Coy.	1		1 9 a.m.			
300 R.F.A.	4		4 1 p.m.	4 x		
D.A.C.	5		5 1 p.m.	5 x		
Hants. Yeo.	1		9 a.m.		1	
Pioneer Btn½	2		2 9 a.m.			
D.H.Q.		1	No. 4 Coy.			
Baggage Section:-						
D.H.Q.	1		No. 4 Coy.			
C.R.A.	1		Out of order.			1
C.R.E.		1			1	
300 R.F.A.	5				1	4
D.A.C.	5		3 Hay 9 a.m.			2
Hants Yeo.	1				1	
Pioneer Btn.	2			2		

x These vehicles go to Aubigny in the morning,
   and also to Units with rations in the afternoon.

PERMANENT TRANSPORT FATIGUES

1 G.S. Wagon to Maroeuil
1 G.S. Wagon to Haute Avesnes
1 L.G.S. Company lines, fatigue
1 G.S. Wagon to No.64, Hermaville
1 G.S. Wagon, water fatigue.
2 G.S. Wagons permanently with Convalescent Camp at
                                                  Hermaville

∅ 2 Lent to O.i/c Baths at Maroeuil

(x)15 With R.A.   ⎫
   3 With Infy Bgdes.   ⎬
   3 Permanently under repair.   ⎭

- WAR DIARY -
60th. (LONDON) DIVISIONAL TRAIN. September 1916.

No. 2 Company 60th. Divl. Train.   GROUP "B"

Transport State, week ending 19-8-16.   Appendix IV.

Units composing Group	Vehicles per Establt.		How working.				
			A To Unit with Supplies		B To Aubigny	C Permanently with Units	D In the pool
	Mark X	L.G.S.	No.	Time of Refill'g			
					-x-		
H.Q. of Company.... Cooks...../	2		2	1.30.p.m.	2	-	-
Baggage	2	-	-	--	-	2	-
Technical	-	1	-	--	-	1	-
Supply Section							
179. Bde. H.Q.	-	1	1	8.30.a.m.	-	-	-
4 Battalions	8	-	8	8.30.a.m.	-	-	-
179 M.G.Co.	1	-	1	8.30.a.m.	-	-	-
2/4th. Field Amb.	1	-	1	8.30.a.m.	-	-	-
2/4th.Fd.Co.R.E.	1	-	1	8.30.a.m.	-	-	-
303rd. Bde.R.F.A.	4	-	4 ∅	1.30.p.m.	4 ∅	-	-
Baggage Section							
179. Bde. H.Q.	1	-	-	--	-	1	-
4 Battalions	8	-	-	--	8	-	-
303rd. Bde. R.F.A.	5	-	-	--	-	1	4

(-x-)   To AUBIGNY in the morning and to the Units with supplies in the afternoon.

∅   4 Wagons go to AUBIGNY in the morning and to Units with Supplies in the afternoon.

PERMANENT TRANSPORT FATIGUES

Town Major..............................2 Wagons
2/4th. R.E. Supplies...................1 Extra Wagon
Trench Mortar B.H.Supplies............1 Wagon
Manure..................................1 Wagon
Ordnance Stores.......................1 Wagon

In addition every two days......1 Wagon goes for vegetables
                                1 Wagon goes for R.E.Stores, etc.

- WAR DIARY -
60th. (LONDON) DIVISIONAL TRAIN. September 1916.

No. 3 Company. 60th. Divl. Train.   GROUP "C"

Transport State, week ending 19.8.16.

Units composing GROUP	Vehicles per Estab.		How working.				
	Mark X	L.G.S.	A. To Unit with Supplies.		B. To Aubigny	C. Permanently with Units.	D. In the pool
			No.	Time of Refill'g.			
H.Q. of Company.							
Cooks	2	-	2	1.30.p.m.	2 @	-	-
Baggage	2	-	-	--	-	2	-
Technical	-	1	-	--	-	1	-
Supply Section							
180.Bde. H.Q.	-	1	1	8.3.0.a.m.	-	-	-
4 Battalions	8	-	8	8.30.a.m.	-	-	-
180.M.G.Co.	1	-	1	8.30.a.m.	-	-	-
2/5th. Field Amb.	1	-	1	8.30.a.m.	-	-	-
1/6th. Field Co.R.E.	1	-	1	8.30.a.m.	-	-	-
302. Bde. R.F.A.	4	-	4 @	1.30.p.m.	4 @	-	-
Baggage Section							
180. Bde. H.Q.	1	-	-	--	-	1	-
4 Battalions	8	-	-	--	8	-	-
302. Bde. R.F.A.	5	-	-	--	-	1	4

@ — These Vehicles go to AUBIGNY in the morning and to Units with Supplies in the afternoon.

The following work is done daily by No. 3 Company from wagons under heading "D" and by working those under heading "A" double journeys:-

Town Major..................1 Wagon
Bde. H.Q. Ordnance
          and Canteen..........1 Wagon.

- WAR DIARY -
60th. (LONDON) DIVISIONAL TRAIN. September 1916.

No. 4 Company, 60th. Divl. Train   GROUP "D"

Transport State, week ending 19.8.16.

Units composing Group	Vehicles per Estab.		How working.			
			A. To Unit with Supplies	B. To Aubigny	C. Permanently with Units	D. In the pool
	Mark X	L.G.S.	No.	Time of Refill'g.		
H.Q. of Company					@@	
Cooks	2	–	2	1.30.p.m.	2	–
Baggage	2	–	–	– –	–	2
Technical	–	1	–	– –	–	1
Supply Section						
181. Bde. H.Q.	–	1	1	8.30.a.m.	–	–
4 Battalions	8	–	8	8.30.a.m.	–	–
181.Bde.M.G.Co.	1	–	1	8.30.a.m.	–	–
2/6th. Field Amb.	1	–	1	8.30.a.m.	–	–
3/3rd.Fd.Co.R.E.	1	–	1	8.30.a.m.	–	–
301 Bde. R.F.A.	3	–	3@@	1.30.p.m.	3@@	–
Baggage Section						
181 Bde. H.Q.	1	–	–	– –	–	1
4 Battalions	8	–	–	– –	8	–
301 Bde. R.F.A.	4	–	–	– –	1	3

@@ These Wagons go to Aubigny in the morning and to Units with Supplies in the afternoon.

PERMANENT TRANSPORT FATIGUES

1 Limber (Technical) with Supply Details daily.

1 G.S. Wagon (Baggage) to D.A.D.O.S. daily.

60TH (LONDON) DIVISIONAL TRAIN, A.S.C.
WAR DIARY — September 1916.
Appendix V

O.C. 1,2,3,4 Coys.
60th. Divl. Train.

Inspection of First Line Transport.

(1) Officers Commanding Divisional Train Companies are responsible to the O.C. Divisional Train for periodical inspections of 1st. Line Transport of all Units in the Group to which their company is allotted.

(2) Thorough inspections of each Unit are to be carried out once a fortnight. Following each fortnightly inspection a report on the lines of the attached pro-forma will be forwarded to this office. In the case of Divisional Troops this report will be forwarded direct, in the case of the Infantry Brigade Units the report will be forwarded through the Headquarters of the Brigade concerned. Particular attention must be paid to Brigade M.G. Coys.

(3) Officers Commanding Divl. Train Coys. must realize their responsibility in regard to the upkeep of vehicles and harness of 1st. Line Transport. By War Establishment an Infantry Battalion is allowed no artificers for this purpose.
The detailing of artificers to inspect 1st. Line Transport is most important in the case of vehicles.

Vehicles.

(1) One wheeler of each Brigade Company will be permanently employed on this work. The O.C. company will provide him with a bicycle when required.

(2) He will be in possession of a complete list of all vehicles of 1st. Line Transport in the Brigade.

(3) He will record in his note book daily the vehicles he has inspected and the repairs he considers require to be carried out.
His book will be initialled daily by his company officer.

(4) The company officer will decide as to whether the repairs are to be carried out:-

(a) By the Unit. It must be borne in mind that the Unit can only carry out the most minor repairs.

(b) By the Divisional Train Company.

(c) By the I.O.M. workshops.
The number of vehicles sent to these workshops must be kept as low as possible.

Harness.

A Saddler N.C.O. will accompany the Company Officer during his fortnightly inspections and will make notes as to repairs required.

Shoeing.

The Staff Sergeant Farrier will accompany the Company Officer during his fortnightly inspection.
Particular attention must be paid to the question of spare shoes.

H. P. Dallas
Colonel,
Commanding,
60th.(London)Divisional Train.

S.T./27/10.
Train Headquarters,
16th. September, 1916.

WAR DIARY.
60TH (LONDON) DIVISIONAL, A.S.C.
PRO-FORMA.

APPENDIX V

Unit.

Date of Inspection

Horses. General condition. State number sick.

Shoeing.

System of feeding and watering.

Condition of lines.

Notes as to animals which the O.C. Unit wishes to cast.

Sufficient Trained shoeing smiths.

Facilities for hot shoeing.

Vehicles.
General condition of woodwork.

Wheels   Washers.

Grease.

Tyres.

Spokes.

Bolts and nuts.

Tailboards.

Poles.

Spare parts.

Brakes.

Harness.

General condition of leather work stitching.

Metal parts.

Stuffing and lining of saddles.

Repairs required.
               (a) Can be done by Unit.
               (b) To be done by company saddler.

War Diary Sept. 1916
60th London Div¹ Train

APPENDIX VI

Groupings of Units for Supplies from 23.9.16 inclusive

Group A
- 60 Div Signal Co
- HQ 60 Div Artillery
- HQ R.E.
- 302 Bde R.F.A.
- 60 DAC
- 1/12. L.N.Lancs (Pioneer) Bn
- HQ & HQ Coy Div Train
- Sanitary Section
- Mob: Vet. Sec
- 155 Coy R.E.
- Div. Baths
- Div. Salvage Coy.
- 21st Reserve Park

Group B Hd 179 Inf Bde
- 7/13. 7/14. 7/15. 7/16 Dns L.Regt
- 179. T.M Battery
- 179. Bde M G Coy
- 303 Bde R.F.A.
- 7/4 Fd Co R.E.
- No 2 Co Div Train
- 7/4 Fd Amblce
- W. 60. T.M Battery

Group C Hdqrs 180 Inf Bde
- 2/7. 2/18. 2/19 & 2/20 Bns L. Regt
- 180. M.G Coy.
- 180 T.M. Battery
- 1/6 Fd Co R.E.
- No 3 Co Div Train
- 2/5 Fd Amblce.
- 176th Tunnelling Co.
- 19th Corps Light Railway
- 47th A.A. Battery
- 147th (A.T.) Coy R.E.

Group D Hdqrs 181 Inf Bde
- 7/21. 7/22. 7/23 & 7/24
- 181. M.G.Coy.
- 181. T.M Batty
- 301 Bde R.F.A
- 3/3 Fd Co R.E.
- No. 4 Coy Div Train
- 1/6 Fd Amblce
- 60th Convalescent Coy.
- X 60 TM Batty
- Y — " —
- Z — " —
- 18th Bn Cheshire Regt
- 30 Div. T.M. Batty
- Div. H.Q.

WAR DIARY Sept 1916
Co London Div Train

APPENDIX VII

Subject
    Regrouping - Refilling, Transport.

OC 1234 Cos.
SSO [...]

From the 29th The attached is the amended Time Table for Refilling
inst.
    Supply Officers must warn the representatives of the
Units concerned, at the Refilling Point tomorrow.
    The Supply Sections working from Railhead should be
composed as nearly as possible from the supply wagons of
Units drawing Supplies at the 2nd Refilling.
    It is hoped by this new scheme to give every driver
& pair of horses one day in the Company lines in every six.
    In order to enable me to keep in touch with the
Transport state of each Company, the Transport Return
due at this office at 6pm daily will be made out on the
attached proforma.
    The same return will show sick horses. The
separate sick horse return will not be required in future.
    This state will only include wagons on the
Company lines.

(Sd) H.G. Seth Smith. Captain
Adjutant
Co Div Train

ST/22/5
In the field
25 Sept 1916

WAR DIARY 60 Lond. Div. Train
SEPTEMBER 1916
APPENDIX VII

Time Table for Loading at Railhead & for Refilling at Dumps
with effect from 29th Sep 1916 inclusive.

Group B.	Group C	Group A	Group D
Loading at Railhead 8.30 am	Loading at Railhead 8.45 am	Loading at Railhead 9.0 am	Loading at Railhead 9.15 am
\multicolumn{4}{c}{First Refilling at Dump}			
8.30 am	8.45 am	9.0 am	9.15 am
HQ 179 Bde Battns in Trenches 179 T.M. Battery 179 M.G. Co W. 60. T.M Battery 147 (A.T.) Co R.E. Town Major ECOIVRES	HQ 180 Bde Battns in Trenches 180 T.M. Battery 180 M.G. Co 110. A.A. Battery	185 Tunnelling Co R.E. Divl. Baths Salvage Co No 1 Sec. Res. Pk Sanitary Section 60 Signal Co HQ. R.A. HQ R.E. Mob. Vet. Sec. Div Anti Gas School 278 Co R.E. 17" Gpo Light Rlwy.	Div. H.Q. HQ 181 Bde Battns in Trenches 181st T M Battery 181st M.G. Co 60 Convalescent Co X/60. T.M. Battery Y/60. ,, Z/60. ,, 18th Cheshire Regt.
\multicolumn{4}{c}{Second Refilling at Dump}			
10.30. am	10.45 am	11. am.	11.15 am
Battns in Rest. 303 Bde R.F.A 2/4 Field Co 2/4 Field Amb. No 2 Co Train	Battns in Rest No. 3 Co Train 2/5 70 Field Ambl. 1/6 70 Co R.E.	No. 1 Co. Train 302 Bde R.F.A 60th DAC 1/12. L.N Lancs Regt (Pioneers).	Battns in Rest No 4 Co Train Train H.Q. 2/6 Field Amb: 3/3rd Field Co R.E. 301 Bde R.F.A

Train HQ
25.9.16. ST/22/5

WAR DIARY. Co. in Transit
April 1916
APPENDIX VIII

Daily Transport State

Company _____

	WAGONS		HORSES		HORSES SICK	
	G.S.	L.G.S.	Riding	H.D.	L.D.	
WITH THE COMPANY						
Detail for Tomorrow						
A						
B						
C						
AVAILABLE FOR TRANSPORT FATIGUES						

NOTE

A. From AUBIGNY to THE DUMP AND FROM DUMP TO UNIT.

B. FOR SUPPLIES 1ST REFILLING

C. PERMANENT TRANSPORT FATIGUES

- WAR DIARY -

60th. (LONDON) DIVISIONAL TRAIN.

September 1916.   Appendix IX

Report of purchases made by Divisional Requisitioning Officer during the month of September 1916.

GREEN FORAGE.

During the month of September, I was unable to find such large fields as during the previous month: and I purchased fields not much larger generally than two to three acres. They were all second crop cuts, either clover, lucerne Sainfoin, or veitch. I think on the whole there was not such a big demand for Green Forage by the Division as during the previous month: this was largely attributable to the bad weather, which lasted throughout the month. The Divisional Ammunition Column, however, received considerable quantities; as I was able to find fields for them close to their horse lines. But it was found impossible by the farmers to do the cutting themselves, as they needed all the labour they could obtain, for bringing their own crops: this too would account for the lack of demand on the part of certain Units, who were unable to find men to do the cutting. Moreover the small reapers issued by Ordnance for this purpose, would appear to be quite inadequate: those Units that managed to borrow scythes cut the crops not only more quickly, but more effectively as with the reapers about 30 per cent is wasted. I endeavoured again as far as possible to make clear the location of fields by the lavish use of sign boards. But in spite of this I found Units continually trespassing on adjoining fields, and in some cases on fields several m miles away. In these cases I went round to the owners of the fields, which had been taken by mistake, and bought them up. As a general rule, this solved the difficulty: and although it is not very satisfactory, I do not see how such misunderstandings can be entirely obviated.

All the farmers with whom I dealt, continued to show me every courtesy; and the prices of the fields were very considerably below the Army Rate.

MEDICAL COMFORTS

The price of eggs remains between 20 and 25 centimes: milk always at 30 centimes. The purchases are made by the Quartermasters of the Field Ambulances, from whom I redeem them once a week.

QUICK LIME

About two tons were purchased during the month for whitewashing and disinfecting.

STRAW

A very small quantity was bought for tying round the box of Wagon wheels, and in two cases for paillasse straw for the Field Ambulances Latterly however Straw came up from Railhead.

Beyond these remarks, I have nothing to note.

(Sgd) V.J. Seligman, 2/Lieut.

- WAR DIARY -

60th. (LONDON) DIVISIONAL TRAIN.

September 1916.   Appendix X.

VEGETABLE STATEMENT.

The following vegetables have been purchased locally during the month:-

CABBAGES..........at 20fcs. per 100 Kilos.
CARROTS..........at 16 "   "   "   "
TURNIPS..........at 10 "   "   "   "

The total amount bought was 54123 Kilos

In consequence of 1½ ozs. of cheese per day being dropped I have recently purchased an extra 2 ozs. of Green Vegetables per man per day and the issue has been made 3 times a week instead of twice as before.

The carrots and turnips are still of a very good quality and the former are being bought below the price fixed by the Government.

The quality of the cabbages improves each time and we are if anything getting rather more than 2 Kilos per cabbage which is the weight at which they are averaged.

I am still perfectly satisfied with the merchants from whom the vegetables are bought and they have always brought up the full quantity ordered.

2-10-16.

(Sgd) F.A.H.Henley, 2/Lieut.
60th. Divisional Train,
R.O. 180th. Brigade.

Vol 5

WAR DIARY
– of –
6th London Div: Train

1st October 1916 to 31st October 1916

Volume I No: 5

Reference Sheet N. LEWS 1/100,000   WAR DIARY 60th (London) Div. Train   Army Form C. 2118

INTELLIGENCE SUMMARY   OCTOBER 1916

Page 1.

Place	Date	Hour	Summary of Events and Information	Remarks and references to Appendices
HAUTE AVESNES	1/-		Composition of 60th Div. Train and locations as follows:—	
			No 1 Headquarters Coy. HAUTE AVESNES.	
			No 2 Coy - ACQ.	
			No 3 - HAUTE AVESNES.	
			No 4 - HAUTE AVESNES.	
			The units of the 60th Division are located as hereto shewn in APPENDIX I.	
			For supply purposes units are now grouped as & shewn in APPENDIX II.	
			Refilling points are as follows :—	
			Group A. On the ARRAS — ST POL road. West of R.Paz ——, point 600 yds N of V in HAUTE AVESNES	
			Group B. → On the ACQ ECOIVRES road about 200 yds. S of Q in ACQ	
			Group C. On the ARRAS — ST POL road West of R.P. 700 yds N of point E in HAUTE — AVESNES.	
			Group D. → on ARRAS — ST POL road West of R.P. 300 yards N of 2nd E in HAUTE AVESNES.	
			Time of refilling for all groups. (a) There units when empty wagons are not	
			working from Railhead 8.30 a.m.	
			(b) When working from Railhead 12 noon.	

(Ref: Sheet 11 LENS 1/100,000) WAR DIARY 60th (London) Div. Train Army Form C. 2118

INTELLIGENCE SUMMARY OCTOBER 1916

Page 2

Place	Date	Hour	Summary of Events and Information	Remarks and references to Appendices
HAUTE AVESNES	1st (Continued)		All supplies are drawn from railhead by Horse Transport. Wagons from the 21st Reserve Park are used to augment divisional transport of the 60th Divisional Train. These are distributed to groups as required. The talk and authorities for drawing from railhead are as shown in APPENDIX III. Supply Section working from railheads are composed as shown in appendix III. This system has been working satisfactorily and leaves about 20 wagons in the "POOL" after all permanent transport fatigues have been furnished. From 1st to 14th October there is nothing of interest to report. All Supply and Transport arrangements have worked satisfactorily and according to time table.	
HAUTE AVESNES	14th		Railhead changed from AUBIGNY to FREVIN CAPELLE. Appendix I shews other lorries for Transport working from railhead. No arrangements orders scheduling lorry transport but lorries are 1½ hour to work from railhead. Appendix VI shews rays. Sketch map of railhead.	

WAR DIARY (Ref. Maps two 11) 60th Divisional Train. Army Form C. 2118

INTELLIGENCE SUMMARY OCTOBER 1916. Page 3

Place	Date	Hour	Summary of Events and Information	Remarks and references to Appendices
HAUTE AVESNES.	14th – 20th	—	No incidents of importance to record all arrangements for supplies and transport have worked smoothly. There have been no changes in the locations of units.	
	20th	—	Instructions received for move of 60th Division to new area and for units here to be handed over to 3rd Canadian Division. O.C. Train 3rd Canadian Division visited Train headquarters and was informed as to working of supplies and all supply arrangements for the Division.	
	22 to 27	—	Orders received from Divisional Head Quarters as to the dates and location of the units of the Division during the move to the new concentration area Divisional Train Orders No. 1 were issued see Appendix VIII and IX and consequent grouping of units see appendix X and also a list of localities of units see appendix X.	
HOUVIN			These orders carried the supply and transport arrangement of the division up to and including the night of the 27/28th October. All supplies were drawn during this period and sent practically as soon as the unit debussed. There were no cases of supply wagons being kept waiting for Bus-train of men and then not.	

Ref map Left 1/40000 **WAR DIARY** 60th Divisional Train Army Form C. 2118

INTELLIGENCE SUMMARY October 1916

Page 4

Place	Date	Hour	Summary of Events and Information	Remarks and references to Appendices
HOUVIN	22 to 27		Unable to join their units. The baggage wagons remained with their units during the whole of this period.	
HOUVIN	27		Orders were received to continue the march South to new area for the night 28/29th October. Arrangements for refilling groupings and the moving of the Companies were made as shown in Appendix XI. Again on this occasion no casualty occurred in the Train and no supplies failed to reach their units during the afternoon of the 28th.	
FROHEN LE PETIT	28		Train Headquarters marched to FROHEN LE PETIT and proceeded on the 29th to BERNAVILLE and remained there till end of month.	
	29.		On the 29th the division continued its march South and orders were accordingly issued to the refilling point groupings marching to their respective Train Companies. All wagons and horses safely reached their respective destinations and supplies were duly delivered. Some lorries however rolled late in arriving owing to the difficulties country that had to be covered especially by the turnout 13 group supply section and some of their train were expectedly clearing up or returning to their lines and evening but were alright the next day.	

Ref Map Lens 1/100,000

WAR DIARY 60th Divisional Train

INTELLIGENCE SUMMARY October 1916

Army Form C. 2118

Page 5

Place	Date	Hour	Summary of Events and Information	Remarks and references to Appendices
BERNAVILLE	29th		All three train companies report safe arrival of their respective supply sections having duly delivered their rations. The last wagon returned to its company lines at 11.30 p.m. that evening. The unit failed to receive its supplies that evening. Baggage wagon horses are recalled from units to be examined & added. The Train is to remain in its present area. All groups remain the same as on Table issued the 29th. See appendix XIII. Refilling takes place at 8.30 A.M. and the last wagon returns its company lines at 3.30 p.m. in the afternoon.	Appendix XIII
BERNAVILLE	30th		The same arrangements were carried out as on the following day. Throughout the whole of the Train there was not a single serious hitch in the supply & transport arrangement carried out by the divisional train and the horses all other than those which for several days can hard and the horses had been accustomed to, remarkably well.	
— —	31st		During the time the Bourbes the Divisional Supply Column came into operation on the 24th October. Railhead was changed to FREVENT on the 26th and to CONTVILLE on the 30th October. On the 31st October Captain H.G. SETH-SMITH leaves the train to take up the duties of D.A.Q.M.G. and 2/Lt RDUMAS is appointed acting adjutant.	

WAR DIARY or INTELLIGENCE SUMMARY

Army Form C. 2118

Ref: Zone II Ypres 60th Divisional Train Page 6

Place	Date	Hour	Summary of Events and Information	Remarks and references to Appendices
General Information			During the month good progress was made with tent flooring & anti-slip. Considerable difficulty is obtaining gravel and other suitable material and at the moment of leaving the area some really good and concrete lines were made. A large amount of building work was also undertaken and anti-rat work completed to the comfort of the men, dining halls, cook houses, larders rooms and every sort of building & improvements considered necessary being erected and at the same time to reduce the work was done by the train wheelers. At the same time to reduce the train and the first line transport was continuously employed and maintained in good running order so that when the men came all vehicles were fit to take the road on except on wagon which was replaced by a new one. The weather was not good on the whole being wet nearly throughout the month. However the health of the men continued good throughout the month the average number sick being 5 daily. The average daily number of H.Q. three Coys. sick for all causes was 20 and of these 75% were reported by the veterinary officer as being capable of work ie. as emergency.	

R. [signature] Major
60TH (LONDON) DIVISIONAL, A.S.C.

APPENDIX I

Location of Units

Right Sector 181st Inf Bde HQ – Etrun
　　　　　　　　Adv HQ – G.9.b.2.9.
　　　　　　　　Res Stn – Etrun
　　　Right Art Group HQ – G.9.b.2.9.
　　　　Batteries A.301 Lanesett　　　　3/30 Fd Co R.E. HQ ANZIN
　　　　　　　　B.301　　–　　　　　　1 Co. Pioneers – ANZIN & LOOEZ
　　　　　　　　C.301　　–
　　　　　　　　D.256　　–
　　　　　　　　B.258 – Thevin Capelle

Centre Sector 179th Inf Bde HQ – Ecoivres
　　　　　　　　Adv HQ – A.8.d.2.5.
　　　　　　　　Res Stn – Bray
　　　Centre Art Group HQ – Madagascar
　　　　Batteries: A.258 Thevin Capelle
　　　　　　　　A.302　Acq　　　　　　2/4 Fd Co R.E. – MARŒUIL
　　　　　　　　B.302　　"　　　　　　1 Co. Pioneers – Ariane
　　　　　　　　C.302　　"
　　　　　　　　D.302　　"
　　　　　　　　D.260 Haute Avesnes
　　　　　　　　C.303 Acq

Left Sector 180 Inf Bde HQ – MONT ST ELOY
　　　　　　　　Adv HQ – A.8.c.7.9.
　　　　　　　　Res Stn – Mont St Eloy
　　　Left Art. Group HQ – BERTHONVAL
　　　　Batteries. C.258 – Thevin Capelle
　　　　　　　　A.303 – Capelle Fermont
　　　　　　　　B.303 –　　　"
　　　　　　　　D.303 –　　　"
　　　　　　　　A.260 – Haute Avesnes
　　　　　　　　B.260　　　"
　　　　　　　　C.260　　　"
　　　1/6 Fd Co R.E. – Mont St Eloy
　　　1 Co Pioneers – Neuville St Vaast

　　HQ Pioneers + 1 Co – Marœuil

SUBJECT:- REFILLING POINTS.

APPENDIX VI
D.A.Q.M.G.
22 SEP 1916
/5/9/2.

C.R.A.
C.R.E.
H.Q. 179th Infy. Bde. "C"
H.Q. 180th -do-   "C"
H.Q. 181st -do-   "C"
O.C. Pioneer Battn.
O.C. 60th Train.
A.D.M.S.
A.D.V.S.
O.C. 60th Signal Coy.
Camp Commandant.
S.S.O.
O.C. D.A.C.
A.P.M.
D.A.D.O.S.
A.P.S.

O.C. No. 1 Sec. 21st Res. Park.
O.C. Mobile Vet. Sec.
O.C. 18th Bn. Cheshire Regt.
O.C. XVIIth Corps Light Rly.
O.C. 60th Convalescent Coy.
O.C. 60th Salvage Coy.
O.C. Divl. Baths
O.C. 147(a.T.) Coy. R.E.

The following Grouping for Supplies will be in force as from the 23rd instant inclusive.

REFILLING POINTS.

"A" GROUP on ARRAS - ST.POL road at HAUTES AVESNES.
"B"   "   on the ACQ - ECOIVRES road East of ACQ.
"C"   "   on the ARRAS - ST.POL road West of HAUTES AVESNES.
"D"   "   on the ARRAS - ST.POL road at HAUTES AVESNES.

TIME OF REFILLING.

"D"   ...   8-0 a.m.
"C" & "B"..   8.30. a.m.
"A"   ...   9.0 a.m.

Except that the following Units will Refill at 1 p.m. instead of 8.30 a.m. :-
   300, 301, 303 Bdes. R.F.A. and D.A.C. and 302nd F A Bde
   Nos. 1, 2, 3, 4 Coys. Divisional Train.

The four Artillery Brigades will continue to draw their Hay at 8.30 a.m.

GROUPING.

GROUP "A".

60th Signal Coy.
H.Q. Divl. Artillery.
H.Q. Divl. Engineers.
302nd Brigade R.F.A.
60th D.A.C.
1/12th L.N.Lancs Pioneer Bn.
H.Q. & No. 1 (Hdqtrs) Coy. Div. Train.
Sanitary Section.
Mobile Veterinary Section.
185th Company R.E.
Divisional Baths.
Divl. Salvage Coy.
No. 1 Sec. 21st Res. Park.

GROUP "B".

H.Q. 179th Infantry Bde.
2/13, 2/14, 2/15, 2/16th London Regts.
179th T.M.Battery.
179th Brigade Machine Gun Coy.
303rd Bde. R.F.A.
2/4th Field Coy. R.E.
No. 2 Coy. Divl. Train.
2/4th Field Ambulance.
V/60 T.M.Battery.

GROUP "C"   GROUP "D".

H.Q. 180th Infantry Bde.   H.Q. 181st Infantry Bde.
2/17,2/18,2/19,2/20th Ldn.Regts.   2/21,2/22,2/23,2/24, Ldn. Regts.
180th Brigade M.G.Coy.   181 Brigade M.G.Coy.
180th T.M.Battery.   181st Bde. T.M.Battery.
1/6th Field Coy, R.E.   301st Brigade L.F.A.
No. 3 Coy, Divl. Train.   3/3rd Field Coy, R.E.
2/5th Field Ambulance.   No. 4 Coy, Divl. Train.
176th Tunnelling Coy, R.E.   2/6th Field Ambulance.
17th Corps Light Rly.   60th Convalescent Coy.
47th A.A.Battery.   X/60 T.M.Battery.
147th (A.T.) Coy, R.E.   Y/60 T.M.Battery.
                                           Z/60 T.M.Battery.
                                           18th Bn. Cheshire Regt.
                                           30th Divl. T.M.Battery.

                                                  B. Barnett
"Q"   Captain.
SEPT. 22nd 1916.   D.A.Q.M.G.

APP. XII III

Subject: Re-grouping, Refilling, Transport.

O.C.,
Nos: 1, 2, 3, and 4 Coss,
A.S.C. for information.

    The attached is the amended Time Table for refilling from the 27th inst.
    Supply Officers must warn the representatives of the units concerned, at the refilling point to-morrow.
    The Supply Sections working from Railhead should be composed as nearly as possible from the supply wagons of units drawing supplies at the 2nd refilling.
    It is hoped by this new scheme to give every driver and pair of horses one day in the Company lines in every six.
    In order to enable me to keep in touch with the Transport state of each Company, the Transport Return due at this office at 6.p.m. daily will be made out on the attached proforma.
    The same return will show sick horses. The separate sick-horse return will not be required in future.
    This state will only include wagons on the Company lines.

                          (Signed.) H.G. SETH-SMITH.

S.T./22/5   Captain.
In the Field.   Adjutant.
25 September 1916.   60th Divisional Train.

Time Table for Loading at Railhead and for Refilling at Dumps.

With effect from 27th Sept 1916. inclusive.

GROUP B.	GROUP C.	GROUP A.	GROUP D.
Loading at Railhead 8.30.a.m	Loading at Railhead 8.45.a.m.	Loading at Railhead 9.0.a.m.	Loading at Railhead, 9.15.a.m.

First Refilling at Dump.

8.30.a.m.	8.45.a.m.	9.a.m.	9.15.a.m.
H.Q. 179th Brigade Battns in Trenches 179th T.M. Batty 179th M.G. Co., W/60 T.M. Batty 147 (A.T.)Co.,R.E. Town Major ECOIVRES	H.Q. 180th Brigade Battns in Trenches 180th T.M. Batty. 180th M.G. Co., 40th Anti-Aircraft Batty.	185 Tunnelling Co.R.E. Divl Baths Salvage Co No.1 Sec. of Reserve Pk Sanitary Sec 60 Signal Co H.Q. R.A. H.Q. R.E. Mobile Vet. Section. Div. Anti-Gas School 278 Co. R.E 17th Corps Light Rally	Divl H.Q. H.Q.181st Brigade Battns in Trenches 181st T.M. Batty 181st M.G. Co., 60 Convalescent Co. X/60 T.M. Batty. Y/60 T.M. Batty. Z/60 T.M. Batty. 18th Cheshire Regt

Second Refilling at Dump.

10.30.a.m.	10.45.a.m.	11.a.m.	11.15.a.m.
Battns in Rest. 303 Bde R.F.A. 2/4th Field Co. 2/4th Field Amb No.2 Co. Train.	Battns in Rest No.3.Co 60 Train 2/5th Field Amb 1/6 Field Co.R.E	No.1 Co 60th Div Train 302 Bde R.F.A. 60th D.A.C. 1/12 L.N. Lancs(Pioneers)	Battns in Rest No.4 Co. Train. Train H.Q. 2/6th Field Amb 3/3 Field Co.R.E 301 Bde. R.F.A.

Train H.Q.
25-9-16.
S.T./22/5.

APPENDIX IV

Composition of Transport Sections
Working from Railhead.

	Unit.	No. of Wagons.
Group. B	Battalion in rest (Supply Wagons)	2
	303 R.F.A. Brigade	4
	No. 2 Coy. Train. (Supply Wagons)	2
	2/4th Field Ambulance (Supply wagon)	1
	2/4th Field Coy. R.E. (Supply wagon)	1
	Baggage wagons of battalions	4
	21st. Reserve Park.	6
		20
Group. C.	Battalion in rest (supply wagons)	2
	No. 3 Coy. Train. (Supply wagons)	2
	2/5th Field Ambulance (Supply wagon)	1
	1/6th Field Coy. R.E. (Supply wagon)	1
	302 R.F.A. (Supply wagons)	4
	Baggage wagons of battalions.	4
	21st. Reserve Park.	5
		19
Group D.	Battalion in rest. (Supply Wagons)	2
	No. 4 Coy. Train (Supply Wagons)	2
	2/6th. Field Ambulance (Supply Wagon)	1
	3/3rd. Field Coy. R.E.	1
	301. R.F.A. Brigade (supply wagons)	4
	Baggage Wagons	5
	21st. Reserve Park.	5
		20
Group. A.	No 1. Coy. (Supply Wagons)	2
	D.A.C. (Supply & hay)	7
	Pioneer Batt.	2
	Divisional Troops (Supply Wagons)	5
	21st. Reserve Park.	12
		28

APPENDIX V

O.C. 1,2,3,4,Cos. 60th Train
O.C. 21st Reserve Park,
SSO, 60th Train

RAILHEAD - 14-10-16

As and from the above date Railhead will be at FREVIN CAPELLE.
Groups will load at the following times:-

    Group D....9.a.m.
           A....9.15.a.m.
           C....9.30.a.m.
           B....9.45.a.m.

Groups D, A, and C, will proceed direct from HAUTE AVESNES to FREVIN CAPELLE Station, and will pick their Reserve Park Wagons at the crossing of the HAUTE AVESNES - FREVIN CAPELLE road, with the ARRAS - ST.POL road, to which corner they will send a mounted N.C.O. to see that the Wagons are ready to join on immediately behind their respective Convoys.

Group B will proceed direct from ACQ to FREVIN CAPELLE and will send a mounted N.C.O. to the crossing of the HAUTE AVESNES - FREVIN CAPELLE road and the ARRAS - ST.POL road to fetch their Reserve Park Wagons which will be waiting there.
Group B will then return to ACQ by the road they came - north of the railway.

Groups, D, A, and C will, after loading, cross the roadway and form up on the road leading to AUBIGNY, and when formed up will proceed to the Dumps following that road, and after again crossing the railway, they will take the first road on the left leading to the ARRAS - ST.POL road, which will bring them on that road just short of "C" Dump.

Officers in charge of Convoys will remember that to be too early is as bad a fault as to be late.

The Reserve Park Wagons will be at the corner stated above twenty minutes before the times for drawing.

Train Hdqrs.
13-10-1916.
S.T./22/7

(sd). R. Dumas.
2/Lieut.
A/Adjutant.
60th (London) Divisional Train.

APPENDIX VI

PLAN OF FREVIN CAPELLE RAIL HEAD.

APPENDIX VI (a)

Regrouping with effect from the 18th Oct 1916.

Group A.

Divl Baths.
Salvage Co.,
No.1.Section Reserve Park.
Sanitary Section.
60th Signal Coy.
C.R.A.
C.R.E.
Mobile Veterinary Section.
Divl Anti-gas School.
278 Co., R.E.
No.1.(H.Q.)Co 60 Train.
17th Corps Light Railway.
301st Bde R.F.A.
302nd Bde R.F.A.
303rd Bde R.F.A.
W. 60th T.M.B.
X 60th T.M.B.
Y 60th T.M.B.
Z 60th T.M.B.
60th Divl Ammn Column.

Group B.

H.Q. 179th Infantry Bde.
2/13th Battn.
2/14th Battn.
2/15th Battn.
2/16th Battn.
179th T.M. Batty.
179th M.G. Coy.
Town Major, Ecoivres.
2/4th Field Co., R.E.
2/4th Field Amb.R.A.M.C.
No.2. Coy Divl Train.

Group C.

H.Q. 180th Infantry Brigade.
2/17th Battn.
2/18th Battn.
2/19th Battn.
2/20th Battn.
180th T.M. Batty.
180th M.G. Coy.
Anti-Aircraft Batty.
2/5th Field Amb. R.A.M.C.
1/6th Field Coy, R.E.
No.3. Coy Divl Train.

Group D.

Divisional Headquarters.
Train Headquarters.
H.Q. 181st Infantry Brigade.
2/21st Battn.
2/22nd Battn.
2/23rd Battn.
2/24th Battn.
181st T.M. Batty.
181st M.G. Coy.
60th Convalescent Coy.
18th Battn Cheshire Regt.
1/12th L.N. Lancs. Regt.
2/6th Field Amb. R.A.M.C.
3/3rd Field Co., R.E.
No.4. Co, Divl Train.

S.S.O.   APPENDIX VII
and Adjutant

Subject: Move.   SECRET.

Headquarters, 179th Infty Bde.   S/S.T/17/2/8.
"   180th "
"   181st "
C.R.E.,
A.D.M.S.
O.C., 60th Divl Signal Co.
1/12th L.N. Lancs. Regt.
A.D.V.S.,
Camp Commandant,
No. 2 Coy Divl Train.
"   3   "
"   4   "

    With reference to Divisional Order No.2 of the 19th inst., the following are the Supply and Transport arrangements during the move.

SUPPLIES.

1. On the day on which units move supplies for the following day will be drawn from the refilling points in this area, in accordance with the time-table now in force.

2. Supplies for the 2/15th, 2/20th, and 2/23rd Battns. London Regt for consumption on the 25th inst. will be sent to their billets direct by lorry on the evening of the 23rd.

3. For other Battalions halting in the TILLOY, PENIN, IZEL-LEZ-HAMEAU area, the arrangements will be as follows:--

    Supply wagons will accompany them filled to this area, carrying rations for the following day. Supply wagons will on the following day accompany the Battalions empty to the new area and will refill immediately on arrival. Representatives of Battalions will be informed by Supply Officers as early as possible, the position of the refilling Point and the Group to which they are allotted.

4. All units will be notified at the refilling points in this area before they move, the groups to which they will be allotted, the position of the refilling points and the times of refilling in the new area.

5. Dumps will be formed in the new area on the 23rd inst. for the following commodities:- Coal, Wood, Straw for billets (where authorised) Green Vegetables (2 ozs. per man) Extra Forage equivalents.
Units before leaving this area should obtain from Supply Officers chits to draw on these dumps. The dumps will be situated as follows:--
            For Group D........ at SARS LE BOIS
            For Groups B and C at MONCHEAUX.
Units drawing coal in their Baggage Wagons should take with them sacks.
Units which take two days to reach the new area should draw two days' supply of these commodities before leaving if they require them, and are able to carry them on the transport available.

available.   (sheet 2.)

6. Headquarters, Divisional Train will open at WAMIN at 12
    noon on the 26th inst. All enquiries in the present area
    after this date should be addressed to O.C., No.1.(H.Q.)
    Coy, Divl Train at HAUTE-AVESNES.

TRANSPORT.

1. No Transport other than that laid down in War Establishments
    can be provided by the Divisional Train during the move.

2. Baggage Wagons will be sent to units by O.C. Divl Train
    Companies at 4.p.m. on the day previous to the day of
    departure.
    They will remain with units until their arrival in the
    new area and the receipt of orders as to their collection.

3. O.C. Units should take steps to report as soon as possible
    to Train Headquarters the breakdown of any Train Transport
    should such occur.

S.O./129/13.   Colonel.
In the Field.   Commanding.
21 Oct. 1916.   60th Divisional Train.

SECRET   APPENDIX VIII   Copy No 8

60th DIVISIONAL TRAIN ORDER, No: 1. (Ref.Sheet 51c.1/40.000)

PART I - Relief of Companies

1. The 60th Division (less Artillery) will be relieved by the 3rd Canadian Division (less Artillery) during the period 23rd to 25th October 1916. The 60th Division will be concentrated in the new Area as shewn in Table "D" by midnight 27th - 28th October 1916.
    Brigade area Commanders are responsible for the allotment of Billets in the area.

2. Divisional Train Companies will be relieved as follows:-

24th. No: 4 Company 60th Div.Train by No: 4 Co.3rd Can.Div.Train.
25th. No: 3 Company 60th Div.Train by No: 3 Co.3rd Can.Div.Train.
26th. No: 2 Company 60th Div.Train by No: 2 Co.3rd Can.Div.Train.
26th H.Q.Company 60th Div.Train by H.Q.Company 3rd Can.Div.Train.

3. O.C.Companies before leaving will hand over their Billets and Lines to the incoming company and will obtain certificates as to cleanliness, as laid down in 60th Divl.Standing Orders. If necessary an officer will be left behind to complete the handing over.

4. Routes to be followed.
No: 4 Company via HERMAVILLE - IZEL LEZ HAMEAU - VILLERS - SIR - SIMON - AMBRING to SARS - LEZ - BOIS.
No: 3 Company via ARRAS - ST POL road - BERLES - PENIN - MAIZIERES - GOUY-EN-TERNOIS - MONTS-EN-TERNOIS to MONCHEAUX.
No: 2 Company. Route and destination as for No: 3 Company.

5. Companies will march each day at 8.30.a.m.

6. Advance parties will proceed before each Company to new area on the day of arrival and will carry out necessary allotment of billets.

7. A lorry will be detailed to each Company on the day of the move to carry surplus stores,kits,etc. Supply Officers must arrange for the use of this Lorry to convey their issuers who are not in possession of Bicycles and surplus supplies remaining on the Dumps to the new Area.
    The Lorry will report to O.C.Company at 7.30.a.m. on the day of the move. This lorry will convey baggage of Train Headquarters in addition to that of No: 2 Company on the 26th instant.
    No Fixtures or Fittings in Billets or Horse Lines are on any account to be moved from the area.

8. Accurate Marching in and marching out States will be rendered in duplicate to this office immediately after a move has taken place.

SECRET 60th Divl. Train Order No: 1 (continued.).

PART II Supply and Transport Arrangements:-

1. Attention is called to this office SECRET S.T./17/2 - "Arrangements for Supplies and Transport during the Move".

2. On the day on which a Unit leaves this area, Supply Wagons will be refilled as usual in this area. The Wagons will then proceed independently direct to the new Billets of that Unit. Where considered necessary O.C. Companies will arrange direct with the Units concerned for the provision of guides.

3. With reference to para.2 (Transport) of this office SECRET S.T./17/2 referred to above, attached Table "A" shews dates of moves of Units of this Division from the present area.

4. Table "B" shews Grouping of Units (This table has been issued direct to Supply Officers by the S.S.O.)
    Refilling Points in the new area are as follows:-

    Groups B & C - On the MONCHEAUX road, head of Refilling point facing South. Order of Groups, -C, B. Head of B. ½ mile clear of MONCHEAUX.

    Group D on the SARS - LEZ - BOIS - MAZIERIES road facing north; head of Refilling point ½ mile clear of the Village of SARS - LEZ - BOIS.

5. Units now drawing Supplies in this area on the 2nd Refilling will draw on the first Refilling on the day of their departure. Supply Officers must inform their Units of this arrangement as soon as possible.

6. Refilling in the new area for all Groups will take place at 8.30.a.m. daily unless otherwise ordered.

? Acknowledge.

Train Headquarters
In the field,
22nd October 1916.

Captain
Adjutant
60th (London) Divisional Train.

Table "A"

POSITION OF UNITS DURING RELIEF

A PRENDIX IE

UNIT	23/24th	24/25th	25/26th	26/27th	27th/28th
Div.H.Q.	HERMAVILLE	-	-	LE CAUROY	-
Salvage Co.	MAROEUIL	-	-	Abolished	-
San.Section.	HERMAVILLE	-	-	LE CAUROY	-
60.Sig.Co.	HERMAVILLE	-	-	LE CAUROY	-
C.R.E.	HERMAVILLE	-	-	LE CAUROY	-
Mob.Vet.Sec.	MAISON ROUGE	-	-	-	GRAND BOURET
H.Q.179.Inf.B.	ECOIVRES	-	-	SIBIVILLE	
2/13th Bn.	C.2	ECOIVRES	ECOIVRES	SAVY	New area
2/14th Bn.	C.1	C.1	MAROEUIL	TILLOY	New area
2/15th Bn.	TILLOY-HERMAVILLE	New area	New area	New area	New area
2/16th Bn.	Bde.Reserve	BRAY	)TILLOY &)HERMAVILLE	New area	-
179.M.G.Co.					
179.T.M.Bty.					
2/4th F.Amb.	ECOIVRES	New area	-	-	-
2/4.Fd.Co.RE	MAROEUIL	Fm.DOFFINE	New area	-	-
No: 2 Co.Train	ACQ	ACQ	ACQ	MONCHEAUX	-
H.Q.180.Inf.B.	MT ST ELOY	-	HOUVIN	-	-
2/17th Bn.	V.1.	Bde.Res.	ECOIVRES	PENIN	-
2/18th Bn.	V.2.	)NEUVILLE)ST VAAST	ACQ	ACQ	New area
2/19th Bn.	BOIS DES ALLEUX	BOIS DES ALLEUX	PENIN	New area	New area
2/20th Bn.	PENIN	New area	-	-	-
180.M.G.Co.					
180.T.M.Bty.					
2/5th F.Amb.	)HAUTE)AVESNES	New area	-	-	-
1/6 Fd.Co.RE	MT ST ELOY	PENIN	New area	-	-
No: 3 Co.Train	HAUTE AVESNES	-	MONCHEAUX	-	-
H.Q.181.Inf.B.	ETRUN	-	BERLENCOURT	-	-
2/21.Bn.	R.1.	R.1.	MAROEUIL	)IZEL LEZ) HAMEAU	New area
2/22.Bn.	R.2.	ETRUN	)IZEL LEZ)HAMEAU	New area	-
2/23.Bn.	)IZEL LEZ) HAMEAU	New area	New area	New area	New area
2/24.Bn.	Bde.Res.	)IZEL LEZ) HAMEAU	New area	New area	New area
181 M.G.Co.					
121 T.M.Bty.					
2/6. Fd. Amb.	)HAUTE)AVESNES	New area	New area	-	-
3/3rd Fd.Co.RE	ANZIN	Fm.DOFFINE	New area	-	-
1/12.L.N.Lanc.	LOUEZ	LOUEZ	Fm.DOFFINE	LIENCOURT	-
No: 4 Co.Train.	)HAUTE)AVESNES	)SARS LEZ) BOIS	-	-	-
Train H.Q.	)HAUTE)AVESNES	-	-	LE CAUROY	-

TABLE "D"

LE CAUROY   -   Div.H.Q.

179 Bde area.   Troops

SIBIVILLE   -   Bde H.Q.   )
BUNEVILLE   )   179.Inf.Bde
MONTS EN TERNOIS   )   2/4 Fd Co.R.E.
MONCHEAUX ½   )   2/4 Fd.Amb.
SERICOURT   )   Det.Train.
HONVAL

   REBREUVE is added to this area for the night og 28-29th.

180 Bde.area   Troops

HOUVIN   -   Bde H.Q.   )
HOUVIGNEUL   )   180 Inf.Bde
CANETTEMONT   )   1/6 Fd.Co.R.E.
MAGNICOURT   )   2/5 Fd.Amb½
MONCHEAUX ½   )   Det.Train.

   REBRUEVIETTE, ROZIERE and BROUILLY are added to this area
for the night of the 28/29th.

181 Bde.area   Troops

BERLENCOURT -   Bde H.Q.   )
MAIZIERES   )   181 Inf.Bde
SARS LEZ BOIS   )   3/3rd Fd.Co.R.E.
DENIER   )   2/6 Fd.Amb.
GOUY EN TERNOIS   )   Det.Train.

ETREE-WAMIN is added to this area for the night of the 28/29th.

LIENCOURT   ....   1/12 L.N.LANCS R.

GRAND BOURET ...   .   )   60.Div.Supply Column.
)   60. Mob.Vet.Sec.

LE CAUROY 60.Div.Train

LE CAUROY   ...   .   60.San.Sec.

@@@@@@@@@@@@@@@@@@@@@@@@@@@@@@@@@@@

APPENDIX X   TABLE B

GROUPING 24.10.16 to 28.10.16.

	24th.	25th.	26th.	27th.	28th.
Divisional Headquarters.	D.	A.	A.	D. B	D. B
Salvage Co.	A.	A.	A.	- B	- B
No.1 Sec.Reserve Park.	A	A	A	A	A
Sanitary Section.	A	A	A	D B	D B
60th Signal Co. X	A	A	A	D B	D B
C.R.A.	A	A	A	A	A
C.R.E.	A	A	A	D B	D B
Mobile Vet Section	A.	A.	A.	A.	B.
Divl Anti-Gas School	A	A	A	B Can	A (X)
278 Co., R.E.					Can
No.1. Co., Divl Train	A	A	A	A	A
17th Corps Light Rely.	A	A	A	A can	A can
H.Q.179th Infty Bde.	B.	B.	B.	B.	B.
2/13th Battalion.	B	B	B	B(a)	B
2/14th "	B	B	B	B(a)	B
2/15th "	B(b)	D	D C	B	B
2/16th "	B	B	C(a)	B	B
No.2. Co.Div.Train.	B	B	B	B	B
2/4th Field Amb.	B	D	D C	B	B
2/4th Field Co., R.E.	B	D(a)	D C	B	B
179th M.G. Coy.	B				
179th T.M. Batty.	B			can	can
Town Major, ECOIVRES.	B	B	B	B A	B A
H.Q.180th Infty Bde.	C	C	C	C	C
2/17th Battalion.	C	C	B	B C	C(a)
2/18th "	C	C	B	A	C.
2/19th "	C	C	C(a)	C	C
2/20th "	C(b)	D	C	C	C
No.3.Co.Div Train	C	C	C	C	C
1/6th Field Co., R.E.	C	D(a)	C	C	C
2/5th Field Amb.	C	D	C	C	C
180th T.M. Batty.	C				
180th M.G. Coy.	C				
62nd Anti-Aircraft Batty		A	A	A can	A can
Train H.Q.,	D	A	A	A	A
H.Q.181st Infty Bde.	D	C	D	D	D
2/21st Battalion.	D	B	B	D(a)	D
2/22nd "	D	C	D(a)	D	D
2/23rd "	D(b)	D	D	D	D
2/24th "	D	D(a)	D	D	D
No.4.Co.Div.Train.	D	D	D	D	D
3/rd Field Co., R.E.	D	D(a)	D	D	D
2/6th Field Amb.	D	D	D	D	D
1/12th L.N. Lancs.	C	C	D(a)	D	D
16th Battn Cheshire Regt	D	A	A	A can	A can
181st T.M. Batty	D	C	D(a)	D	D
181st M.G. Coy.	D	C	D(a)	D	D
60th Convalescent Co.	Included in Div: H.Q.				
519th How. Bde R.F.A.	A ←——————→ A ←——————→ A
301st Bde. R.F.A.	
302nd Bde. R.F.A.	
303rd Bde. R.F.A.	
60th Divl Ammn. Col.	A ←——————→ A ←——————→ A
W 60th T.M.B.	
X 60th T.M.B.	
Y 60th T.M.B.	
Z 60th T.M.B.	A ←——————→ A ←——————→ A

X. Details moving before 26th will be rationed from Group A
(X) Unless previously closed.
(a) Proceed to new area with mid-and refill on arrival with rations for next day's consumption.
(b) Supplies for 25th direct to unit in billets by Lorry on evening of 23rd.

APPENDIX IV

SECRET

Copy No 11

Div: Train A.S.C.
27 OCT. 1916
No. S.T/11/21

60th London Divisional Train
Order No 2

1. The 60th Divl Train less Headquarters Coy will move to the new area to-morrow the 28th inst.

2. The troops of the 60th Division will be accomodated in the New Area the night of the 28/29 October as shewn on attached table (A.)

3. Refilling for groups B. & C will take place on the MONCHEAUX – HOUVIN road at 8.30 A.M.: Refilling must be completed by 10 A.M. and all wagons lashed down and ready to move. Both groups will refill facing S.

4. Headquarters of Nos 2 and 3 Coys will march at the head of their respective Supply Sections and will pass the refilling point at 9.30 A.M. and halt 500 yards clear of refilling points on the MONCHEAUX-HOUVIN road.

5. Routes for B and C Supply Sections will be as follows:-
No 2 Coy via Frevent – VACQERIE-LE-BOUCQ to FORTEL from this point Supply Wagons will proceed to Units and will be collected at FROHEN LE PETIT Headquarters of No 2 Coy to FROHEN LE PETIT direct.
No 3 Coy via. FREVENT – BONNIERES.
At this point Supply Wagons will proceed to Units and will be collected at FROHEN LE PETIT. Headquarters of No 3 Coy to FROHEN LE PETIT direct.

6. Refilling for group D will take place at 4.30 p.m. to-day Supply Wagons returning to their Company lines when refilled

7. Route of Headquarters of No 4 Coy and Supply Section will be as follows:-
IVERNY - LE - SOUICH - BOUQUEMAISON NEUVILLETTE.
From this point Supply Wagons will proceed to Units and will be re-collected at OCCOCHES Headquarters of Company to FROHEN LE PETIT direct.

8. Train Headquarters will close at HOUVIGNEUL at 8 A.M. and will re-open at FROHEN LE PETIT at 12 NOON.

9. Baggage Wagons will remain with Units during this move and until further orders.

10. Refilling point for the 29th will be at the AUXI LE CHATEAU — DOULLENS road.
Group B — Head of R.P. 1 mile W of FROHEN LE GRAND.
Groups D & C in order D - C facing East head of D group dump 2 miles east of FROHEN LE GRAND church

11. Time of refilling on the 29th will be notified later.

12. Supplies for refilling on 29th will be dumped at 3.30 p.m. on the 28th instant.

13. Acknowledge.

B F Dalbiac Colonel
Commanding
60th (London) Divisional

Copy No _____

1 — OC No 2 Coy Train
2 — O.C No 3 Coy Train
3 — O.C. No 4 Coy Train
4 — HQ 179 Bde.
5 HQ 180 Bde.
6 HQ 181 Bde.
7 SSO
8 H.Q. 60th DIV.
9. O.C. 60 DIV SUPPLY COL
10. WAR Diary
11. File

TABLE -A.-

Troops	Area
DIV. H.Q.	(FROHEN LE GRAND
60 San. Sec	(FROHEN. LE PETIT
Det. Train	
60 Mob. Vet. Sec.	
179 Inf. Bde	VILLERS L'HOPITAL - FORTEL -
2/4 Fd. Co. R.E.	BOFFLES - NOEUX - WAVANS -
2/4 Fd. Amb.	
Det. Train	BEAUVOIR WAVANS - BEAUVOIR RIVIERE - BEALCOURT - St. ACHEUL
Bde. H.Q.	WAVANS
180 Inf. Bde.	BONNIERES - REMAISNIL -
1/6 Fd. Co. R.E.	MEZEROLLES - OUTRE BOIS
2/5 Fd. Amb.	
Det Train	
Bde. H.Q.	REMAISNIL
181 Inf. Bde	NEUVILLETTE - BARLY - OCCOCHES
3/3 Fd. Co. R.E.	RANSART.
2/6 Fd. Amb.	
Det. Train	
Bde. H.Q.	OCCOCHES.
1/12 LN. LANCS. R.	CANTELEUX and BEAUVOIR
H.Q.	CANTELEUX
DIV. H.Q.	Will be at FROHEN LE GRAND

APPENDIX XII   Copy No 11

60th Div: Train A.S.C.
28 OCT. 1916
No. S.T/17/34

60th (London) Divl Train Order No 3

1. The 60th Divn (less Artillery) continues its Move S. on 29.10.16.
2. The troops of the 60th Division will be accomodated in the new area on the night of the 29th/30th as shown on attached Table "A".
3. Refilling for groups as follows:-

    B. C and D will be as detailed in Divl Train Order No 2 para 10 of 27.10.16.

    Time of Refilling for all Groups — 8.30 a.m.
    Column will dump at 7.0 am.

    Supply Sections will move on to the Refilling points as follows:-

    No 2 Co from Wagon Park via X roads 100 yards N of church FROHEN-LE-PETIT. Cross roads FROHEN-LE-GRAND N.W. on to Refilling Point.

    No 4 Coy from present Wagon Park via cross roads N of church FROHEN-LE-PETIT. Cross roads FROHEN-LE-GRAND. S.E. on DOULLENS road to Refilling Point.

    No 3 Co. from OUTREBOIS via MEZEROLLES. Wagons to reverse on road junction ½ mile S. of 'A' in FROHEN-LE-GRAND.

    Refilling to be completed by 10.am.

    After Refilling, as soon as Supply Sections are formed up, they will move as follows:-
    No 2 Co Starting Pt — ST ACHEUL — 10.45 am.
    No 3 Co   "   " — rd junction N end of LE MEILLARD — 11-15 am
    No 4 Co   "   " — "   "   S. end of OUTREBOIS — 11.0 am.

4. Distributing points for Wagons will be as follows:-
    No 2 Co — MONTIGNY LES JONGLEURS re collecting point — PROUVILLE
    No 3 Co — LE MEILLARD   re-collecting point — BERNAVILLE
    No 4 — OUTREBOIS

    recollecting point will be at the Billets allotted to No 4 Coy by 181 Bde H.Q.

    Headquarters of Cos will move with their Supply Sections joining them at the starting points.

APPENDIX XIII Grouping 29.10.16

B. Group
Divisional Hdqrs.
Salvage Co
Sanitary Sec
60 Signal Co
C.R.E.
Mobile Vet. Sec.
H.Qrs 179 Infy Bde
2/13 Battn
2/14 "
2/15 "
2/16 "
No 2 Co Div. Train
2/6 Field Ambce
2/6 Field Co R.E.
179 M.Gun Co
179 T.M. Batty
Train Hdqrs.

C. Group
H.Qrs 180 Infy Bde
2/17 Battn
2/18 "
2/19 "
2/20 "
No 3 Co Div Train
2/7 Field Co R.E.
2/5 Field Ambce
180 T.M. Batty
180 M.Gun Co

D Group
Hd Qrs 181 Infy Bde
2/21 Battn
2/22 "
2/23 "
2/24 "
No 1 Co Div Train
2/5 Field Co R.E.
2/8 Field Ambce
1/12 L.N. Lancs
181 T.M. Batty
181 M.Gun Co

Vol 6

Confidential

War Diary of 60th Divl. Train

From 1st November 1916   To: 30th November 1916

Vol: 2   No: 6.

30th November 1916.
W.D. 1

Reference Maps
LENS & HAZEBROUCK 1/100,000
BÉTHUNE & BÉVILLE 1/40,000

WAR DIARY

60th London Division (? 2nd Line)

INTELLIGENCE SUMMARY
(Erase heading not required.)

NOVEMBER 1916

Place	Date	Hour	Summary of Events and Information	Remarks and references to Appendices
BERGUETTE	1st		Headquarters Company and attached in the original area N.W. of ARRAS. The Divisional Supply Column are working out as trains in experience in delivery supplies to any of the units.	
	2nd		The same conditions prevail and no further have taken place in the division.	
	3rd		The Division again moves westwards on the 3rd and 4th - see Appendix I. The march is carried out satisfactorily and no units fail to obtain their rations in good time in either day. On the 4th the Division in arrive in the Lumbres area central area ALLOUAGNE & CLOCHER.	Appendix I
ALLOUAGNE and CLOCHER	4th	9.10 P.M	On the evening of this day the Division is officially informed that it will proceed to SALONIKA and are to be reorganised as far as possible on this side previous to WE. SALONIKA part 4. The organisation to be evening to far as the divisional train is concerned is Frontline and 1st Echelon as readiness of 20 Officers & 1750 O.R.	

Army Form C. 2118.

Reference Map
LENS } 1/40000
AFFREVILLE

WAR DIARY
or
INTELLIGENCE SUMMARY.
(Erase heading not required)

60th London Divisional Train
NOVEMBER 1916

Place	Date	Hour	Summary of Events and Information	Remarks and references to Appendices
AILLY le HAUT CLOCHER	5th		All baggage wagons, horses and drivers are ready for their units for the 3 Brigade Companies and Rendez into the Advanced Horse Transport depot AFFREVILLE as complete turnouts.	See Appendix 3 2 and
	6th		All supply wagons of the Brigade Companies are handed to units as complete turnouts to enable them to have their transport of their Command, and the L.G.S wagons formerly in these Companies are taken over by the Brigade Companies as complete turnouts.	
		7th	Brigade Companies carry out the delivery of supplies with the L.G.S wagons taken over now by the Companies.	
		8th	Rations particulars 7.a/c are tire done on this day.	
		9th	A Commencement was made with the exchange of L.D horses 1/1c division to make with the 2nd Indian Army Reserve Park. This is done in the afternoon so as not to interfere with the working of the Company's ordinary actions in the morning. This is done by No 2 Company 4 the horses heavy and curier out late entirely.	Appendix 4.

WAR DIARY
or
INTELLIGENCE SUMMARY

Army Form C. 2118

80TH (LONDON) DIVISIONAL, A.S.C.

November 1916

Place	Date	Hour	Summary of Events and Information	Remarks and references to Appendices
AILLY LE HAUT CLOCHER	10"		The remainder of the LD horses of the train were exchanged for mules with the 1st & 2nd Indian Cavalry Reserve Park	
	11"		On the way reinforcement of 1000 all ranks arrived at RADINVAL and were taken over by the train: they were divided up between the 4 companies of the train and the Field Ambulances.	Appendix 5
	12"		Officers joined the train & for attached appointments. Three were evacuated sick the day after joining.	
	13"		64 L.G.S. wagons with pairs of mules & harness were drawn on to the D.A.C. It was to make them hand up to strength on of the D.A.C. it was to make that hand up to strength of the the mules took over the supplies of This rendered the train useless for work and the delivering by the 15" & 2" of the division was on after this date	
	14"		Indian Cavalry Reserve Parks Captain C.E. Davis took over the duties of adjutant of the train on this date. All mules of the train were withdrawn for farriers on this & the following day. 37 L.G.S. wagons were handed over complete turnouts to the D.A.C. others completing that unit. By the time the train had practically	

WAR DIARY or INTELLIGENCE SUMMARY

Army Form C. 2118

60TH (LONDON) DIVISIONAL, A.S.C.

November 1916

Place	Date	Hour	Summary of Events and Information	Remarks and references to Appendices
AILLY LE HAUT CLOCHER	15th		The first entraining orders were issued that concerned the Division and the 1st party of the Train left in Train No. 14 on the 17th and in Train No. 15.	
	16th		A further and final reinforcement of O.R.'s all ranks arrived at ABBEVILLE on this day and was taken on by the Train. This completed the train so far as personnel was concerned excepting certain details of No 1 Company for the MOUNTAIN Artillery Brigade, Pioneer Battalion, Cavalry Squadron and Cyclist Company of other units the Train and not Mobilized.	
	17th		After this date reorganizing when time permits interval the Train 20 Transport left to work with on this day 5 officers + 167 other ranks entrained at LONGPRE for MARSEILLE with 92 animals + 4 vehicles	
	18th		10 officers + 200 other ranks + 53 animals + 34 vehicles entrained on this day for MARSEILLE	
	19th		Nothing occurred on this day of special note	

WAR DIARY
80TH (LONDON) DIVISIONAL, A.S.C. — INTELLIGENCE SUMMARY
November 1916

Army Form C. 2118.

Place	Date	Hour	Summary of Events and Information	Remarks and references to Appendices
M.L.D. I.F.M.T. COLUMN	20th		The officer commanding Pack Echelon & the advance left by Passenger Train to take command of Train on it's arrival at SALONIKA.	
	21st		Also on this day 2 officers, 24 other ranks, 21 animals & 9 vehicles entrained.	
			On this day 3 officers & 300 other ranks, 47 animals & 13 vehicles entrained.	
	22nd		On this day 5 officers & 100 other ranks, 67 animals, 9 vehicles entrained.	
	23rd		On this day 4 officers & 3 other ranks, 24 animals, 6 wheeled entrained.	
	24th		On this day 5 officers & 216 other ranks, 21 animals & 5 vehicles entrained. This	
	25th		On this day 7 officers & 421 other ranks 32 animals entrained. This party with entire Train Headquarters and completed the entrainment of the Div. and Train from LONGPRÉ.	
	27th		Train Headquarters arrived at MARSEILLE	
	29th		Major ORELL commanding the Pack Echelon arrived at SALONIKA & opened Train Headquarters there. The only personnel arriving at the same time being one Supply officer & Supply clerk. & one Transport manager for 4 other supplies to the troops that came in the above Transport. (S.S. MEGANTIC) and the local work of the train was satisfactorily carried out.	

WAR DIARY
60TH (LONDON) DIVISIONAL, A.S.C.
INTELLIGENCE SUMMARY.

Army Form C. 2118.

November 1916

Place	Date	Hour	Summary of Events and Information	Remarks and references to Appendices
SALONIKA	30th		S.S. TRANSYLVANIA transport arrived with the divisional Ammunition party on board & Mon Troops. The same method of using local transport was continued and all necessary supplies were issued the day previous to consumption. The main bulk of the A.S.C. ready to deliver supplies to the Troops, was carried out without any serious breakdown under very difficult conditions on several occasions particularly for the first few days at SALONIKA when the divisional camp is situated about 8 miles from the Town & no means of communication at first existed and the nearest telephone was three & a half miles away at the main supply depot. The Base Authorities however did everything possible to help and all Transport required was in most readily provided.	

R.S. Dumas
Lieut Colonel
60th Divl ASC

60TH DIVISIONAL TRAIN ORDER NO. 5.   Appendix II

Reference LENS 11
and ABBEVILLE 1/100,000   SECRET.

ALC

60TH (LONDON) DIVISIONAL, A.S.C.
War Diary
Nov: 1916.

1. The 60th Division moves westward on the 3rd and 4th November, 1916.

2. Refilling on the 3rd will take place at the same points as on the previous days at 8-30 a.m. The Supply Column will dump at 7 a.m. After refilling, Supply Sections will return to their Company lines and march with the Headquarters of their respective Companies to the new areas.

3. Companies will march at 10-30 a.m. in accordance with instruction received from their Brigade Headquarters.

4. Refilling on the 4th instant will take place as follows at 8-30 a.m.

"B" Group on ABBEVILLE - AMIENS Road Head of Refilling Point facing west 300 yards clear of western end of AILLY des CLOUCHES

"C" Group on ABBEVILLE - AMIENS Road head of Refilling Point facing south east 500 yards clear of western end of AILLY des CLOUCHES.   EASTERN

"D" Group on BERNAVILLE - FIENVILLERS Road facing east head of Refilling Point at V in BERNAVILLE

5. Refilling on the 5th instant will take place at 8-30 a.m. as follows

"B" Group same as for 4th instant.

"C" Group same as for 4th instant.

"D" Group on ABBEVILLE - AMIENS Road head of refilling point facing south east 800 yards clear of eastern end of AILLY des CLOUCHES.

6. The Supply Column will dump at 7 a.m. at the above dumps each morning until further notice.

7. Regrouping
There willbe no change on the 3rd 4th; the 5th November the I/12th Loyal North Lancs Battn. will change from "D" Group to "C" Group; otherwise there will be no changes in grouping until further notice.

8. No. 4 Company of the Train will march on the 3rd instant to BERNAVILLE under orders of the 180th Infantry Brigade, and on the 4th instant will march to new area westwards, refilling each morning at the above stated points.

9. Baggage waggons will remain with their Units until further notice.

10. Supply Sections will be despatched to their Units, and re-collected at points in the new area to be arranged by their Company Commanders.

11. No horses that can possibly move are to be left behind.

In the Field.
2nd November, 1916.

2/Lt.
A/Adjutant, 60th Train

Appendix 2
S.T.9/5/2
Copy No. 12

60TH (LONDON) DIVISIONAL, A.S.C.

Reorganisation Order No. 2

War Diary Nov. 1916

O.C. Nos. 2,3 and 4 Cos 60th Train

With reference to Divisional letter Q/242/5 a copy of which was sent you this morning with my S.T.9/5/1 of to-day, the following are the instructions for the 6th and 7th instants:-

NOV.6th (a) - You will expedite the delivery of Supplies as much as possible so as to get the Supply Wagons at an early hour. They need not necessarily return to the Company Lines, provided that they go out complete in the morning.

O.i/c Supply Sections will arrange to rendezvous the following wagons and water carts at the "O" in BELLANCOURT on the ABBEVILLE-FRANCE AMIENS road as early as possible.

EACH COMPANY -	Mark X		
Co. Supply Wagons	2	Field Co RE	1
4 Inf. Battns	8	Bde HQ Co.	1
Bde HQ Extra Forage	1	Water Cart	1
Field Ambulance	1		

Having collected the above vehicles, the O.i/c will proceed to the advanced MT Depot, ABBEVILLE and hand over complete turns-out, retaining drivers and receipts for Wagons. He will at the same time draw 3 Limbered GS Wagons, complete turns-out with drivers, and return to his Company Lines with the 3 Limbered GS Wagons and all drivers of wagons handed in.

(b) - O. C. Companies will arrange with their Bde HQ, Field Ambulances, and Field Cos.RE to receive the Vehicles named in Divll. letter Q/242/5 during the afternoon, complete with Equipment & drivers where stated.

On the night of the 6th, each Bde Co. will then have on its lines the following transport:-

	Vehicles	Mules or LD
From Inf. Bde HQ, L.G.S.Wagons	1	2
4 Battalions	36	72
Bde HQ Co. with teams	8	28
with pairs	4	8
Field Ambulances	4	8
Field Cos RE (without dvr)	1	2
Supply Tech. Eqpt.	1	2
Bde HQ Supplies	1	2
Bde HQ Co.	1	2
Total LGS Wagons	57	126
and 3 L.G.S.drawn from MT Depot	3	12
	60	138

NOV.7th - Supplies will be delivered to Units by such numbers of those LGS Wagons as O.C.Co consider in consultation with their Supply Officers, consider necessary.

RATIONS - All turns-out received with animals must bring with them rations up to and including the night of the day following that on which they are received, and supplementary indents must be immediately forwarded for the increased number of animals for the following day.

Train HQ
5-11-1916.

R. Snow
2/Lieut
A/Adjutant
60th Divisional Train....

Copy No: 1 to CO. 2 Co. Train	Nos: 7	- GHQ
2 " 3 "	8	AHQ
3 " 4 "	9	HQ(Q)
4 179th Bde	10	SSO
5 180th Bde	11	Adv.MT Depot ABBE-
6 181st Bde	12	File VILLE
	13	War Diary

APPENDIX 3

60TH (LONDON) DIVISIONAL, A.S.C.

S.T.9/5/2a

60th Divl. Train Waltham Nov 8 1916

Amendment to Reorganisation Order No: 2

O.C. 2,3, and 4 Cos 60th Trd n

Reference reorganisation Order No: 2 No: ST.9/5/2 of to-day arrangements for Nov 8th para (a) are cancelled and the following substituted.

Dir is ional Train Brigade Companies will hand over to Unit's Supply Wagons, complete turnout less drivers. These will be retained by Units and will be handed in to the Advanced HT Depot immediately prior to entrainment. Divisional Train will take over 1st Line LMS Wagons as previously arranged.

R[signature]
Capt
A/Adjutant
60th Divisional Train

Train HQ
6-11-1916

2 paras (a) b lwr

"A" Form.
MESSAGES AND SIGNALS.

Army Form C.2121
(in pads of 100).
No. of Message ....

Prefix ...... Code ...... m.	Words	Charge	This message is on a/c of:	Recd. at .... m.
Office of Origin and Service Instructions.	Sent		.... Service.	Date ....
....	At .... m.			From ....
....	To			By ....
	By		(Signature of "Franking Officer.")	

TO { ~~179 Bde~~ ~~160~~ ~~181~~ 60 TRAIN

| Sender's Number. | Day of Month. | In reply to Number. | AAA |
| * Q242/5/1 | 5 | | |

Ref my number Secret Q242/5 of 4 November aaa Arrangements for Nov 6 (a) are cancelled and the following substituted aaa Div Train Pack coys will hand over to units supply wagons complete turnout less drivers aaa These will be returned by Units and will be handed in to Adv HT Dept immediately prior to entrainment aaa Div Train will take over the L.S. L.G.S wagons as previously arranged. aaa

By hand.

DS

From
Place — 60 DIV Q
Time 12.40 pm

The above may be forwarded as now corrected.   (Z)
Censor.   Signature of Addressor or person authorised to telegraph in his name.
* This line should be erased if not required.
750,000. W 2186—M509. H. W. & V., Ld. 6/16.

BH.

S E C R E T.

H.Q. 179th Infy. Bde.
H.Q. 180th   do.
H.Q. 181st   do.
O.C. 60th Train.
A.D.M.S.
A.D.V.S.
D.A.D.O.S.
"A" Branch.
"G"   "
D.D.T. of B.H.Q. (For information).

Q/242/5.
4- NOV. 1916
60th LONDON DIVISION

In connection with the reorganisation of this Division for service overseas the following adjustments of Horse Transport will be made on the dates shown:-

NOVEMBER 4th.
O.C. Divisional Train will arrange to collect all Baggage and Supply Wagons from Units of the three Infantry Brigades and Machine Gun Companies.

NOVEMBER 5th.
O.C. Divisional Train will arrange to hand in to Advanced H.T.Depot, ABBEVILLE, all Baggage Wagons of the three Brigade Companies of the Divisional Train. Wagons will be handed in as complete turns-out less Drivers. All wagon equipment will be handed in.

O.C. Divisional Train will arrange direct with the Commandant, Advanced H.T.Depot, time and details of handing over.

NOVEMBER 6th.

(a) O.C. Divisional Train will arrange to hand in all Mark X G.S.Supply wagons and Water carts of Brigade Companies to Advanced H.T.Depot (Supply wagons complete turns-out less Drivers, Water carts vehicles only). This will include the wagons of R.E. Companies and Field Ambulances on strength of Headquarters Company and now attached to Brigade Companies. These wagons will be collected after supplies have been delivered to Units and will proceed to ABBEVILLE after collection; Drivers will return to the Divisional Train Companies.

Wagons will be handed over complete with horses and all wagon equipment.

O.C.Divisional Train will draw from Advanced H.T.Depot, 24 L.G.S.Wagons complete turns-out.

(b) On the afternoon of the 6th instant Infantry Brigades will arrange to send to their respective Divisional Train Coys all L.G.S. wagons, First Line Transport, complete turns-out, with all wagon equipment. Drivers will return to their Units after handing over is completed. This will include Brigade M.G.Coys and Brigade Headquarters. Brigade Machine Gun Companies will hand over teams of four Mules complete with harness.

NOVEMBER 7th.
O.C.Divisional Train will arrange to draw supplies from refilling points and deliver same to Units with the L.G.S. Wagons taken over from the First Line Transport.

The undernoted Table shows the First Line Transport to be taken over by each Brigade Company of the Divisional Train, complete with horses or mules(less Drivers).

(-2-)

Infantry Bde. Headquarters L.G.S.Wagons	...	1.
Each Battalion, 9 L.G.S.Wagons.	...	36
Brigade M.G.Coy, L.G.S.Wagon Teams 8.	...	8.
Pairs.	...	4.
TOTAL.		49.

Brigade Companies of Divisional Train will also take over complete with Drivers, horses and all equipment from Field Ambulance:-

L.G.S.Wagons.	... ...	4
From Field Coy. R.E. L.G.S.Wagons (Without Driver)		1.

The following Train Transport will be retained by Brigade Companies of the Train :-

Wagons L.G.S. for Technical Equipment	...	1.
" " " Supplies for Bde.H.Q.	...	1.
" " " " " Bde.M.G.Coy.		1.

R.P.

"Q"

NOVEMBER 4th 1916.

Captain.

for D.A.Q.M.G.

S E C R E T.

C.R.E.
H.q. 179th Infy. Bde.
O.C. 60th Signal Coy.
O.C. 60th Train.
A.D.M.S.
A.D.V.S.
D.D.T. (Southern Area)
A.D.O.S.

APPENDIX 4
WAR DIARY. NOV. 1916
Q/242/14.

60TH (LONDON) DIVISIONAL, A.S.C.

The attached copy of letter received from G.H.Q. No.Q/5885 dated 2nd instant, is forwarded for your information and necessary action.

With reference to para 2 the following adjustments of L.D.Horses and mules with the 2nd Indian Cavalry Reserve Park will take place on the morning of the 9th instant, exact time and place to be notified later.

(1)   UNIT.   L.D.HORSES for MULES.

Unit	L.D. Horses for Mules
1/6th Field Co.R.E.	25
2/4th -do-	48
3/3rd -do-	24
2/4th Fld. Amb.	17
No.2 Coy. Divl. Train.	All L.D.Horses in possession. Exact numbers to be notified this office by 6 p.m. on the 8th instant.

(2) All wheel harness will be exchanged with the animals.

(3) When teams of 4 L.D. horses complete with harness can be exchanged for teams of four mules this will be done.

(4) Authority has been asked for pairs of L.D.Horses with wheel harness to be exchanged for pairs of mules with lead harness, the decision will be notified to Units concerned.

(5) To adjust the number of animals with the Division the following transfers of Mules will take place on the afternoon of the 9th instant.

(a) Each of the three Field Co.s R.E. will hand over to its affiliated Brigade Coy of the Divisional Train all surplus mules complete with harness together with any surplus sets of harness.

(b) O.C. No.2 Coy. Divisional Train will complete the 2/4th Field Ambulance to 44 Mules, 10 teams of 4 complete with harness and 4 spare mules.

(6) The above mentioned Units will render to this office in triplicate, by 12 noon on the 10th instant a return on the attached proforma "A". The 179th Infantry Bde. will render their return separately by Units.

(7) All animals will be transferred from one Unit to another with headcollars, horse rugs and saddle blankets.

(8) Indents for riding horses to complete to Establishment Part XII will be submitted immediately to A.D.V.S. through this office.

(9) Instructions follow as to the disposal of surplus vehicles.

"Q"
NOVEMBER 6th 1916.

H.G. SETH SMITH.
Captain.
for D.A.Q.M.G.

Appendix 5.
War Diary
Nov 1916

Roll of Officers arriving to join
60TH (LONDON) DIVISIONAL, A.S.C.

Name of Officer	Date joined
Capt. C. E. Davis	12.11.16
Major A. J. Birch	22.11.16
Major J. C. Okell	9.11.16
Capt. J. N. Reeves	11.11.16
Lt. L. W. Hughes	9.11.16
Lt. F. A. P. G. Gore	16.11.16
2/Lt. C. A. Mair	15.11.16
2/Lt. R. W. Hellis	19.11.16
2/Lt. T. B. Quin	16.11.16
2/Lt. A. H. H. Clarke	11.11.16
2/Lt. S. S. Barnard	12.11.16
Lt. R. E. P. Gibson	11.11.16
Lt. J. C. Smith	23.11.16
2/Lt. C. K. Wood	6.11.16
Lt. J. Prescott	19.11.16
2/Lt. C. R. Priestly	13.11.16
2/Lt. R. P. Eykyn	12.11.16